A Multimedia Literacy Project Toward Biblical Literacy in
Bangladesh

TERESA CHAI

Wipf and Stock Publishers
199 W 8th Ave, Suite 3
Eugene, OR 97401

A Multimedia Literacy Project Toward Biblical Literacy in Bangladesh
By Chai, Teresa
Copyright © 2020 APTS Press All rights reserved.
Softcover ISBN-13: 978-1-7252-8615-3
Hardcover ISBN-13: 978-1-7252-8614-6
eBook ISBN-13: 978-1-7252-8616-0
Publication date 8/17/2020
Previously published by APTS, 2020

Publisher's Preface

We are pleased to offer this sixth title in our APTS Press Monograph Series. This is the publication of the author's doctoral dissertation done through Fuller Theological Seminary in Pasadena, California, USA. The purpose of this series is to give our readers broader access to good scholarship that would otherwise be unavailable outside of the academic community. This is part of our ongoing commitment to discipleship through publishing.

The other five titles in this series, *Theology in Context: A Case Study in the Philippines*, by Dave Johnson, *Leave a Legacy: Increasing Missionary Longevity*, by Russ Turney, *Understanding the Iglesia ni Cristo*, by Anne Harper, *A Theology of Hope: Contextual Perspectives in Korean Pentecostalism*, by Sang Yun Lee, and *Business In Islam: Contextualizing Mission in Muslim-Majority Nations*, by Robert J. Stefan, are all available at www.aptspress.org. If you have any questions, you can reach us through our website. We would be happy to hear from you.

We hope you enjoy this book. Please feel free to communicate with us through our website.

THE PUBLISHER

Table of Contents

Publisher's Preface	iii
Preface	xii
Foreword	ix
Dedication	xi
Acknowledgments	xiii
List of Tables	xv
List of Figures	xvi
List of Abbreviations	xvii
Definition of Phrases	xix
CHAPTER 1: Introduction	1
CHAPTER 2: The Challenge of Illiteracy	7
CHAPTER 3: Adult Literacy Theory and Practice	25
CHAPTER 4: Historical Aspects and Influences	39
CHAPTER 5: Religious Aspects and Influences	45
CHAPTER 6: Sociopolitical and Cultural Aspects and Influences	57
CHAPTER 7: Educational and Media Aspects and Influences	65
CHAPTER 8: Communication in Translation as Used in the Bangladesh Literacy Project	71
CHAPTER 9: Using Media to Communicate Scriptures	83
CHAPTER 10: The Experimental Literacy Project in Bangladesh	97
CHAPTER 11: Literacy Materials and Extended Testing	111
CHAPTER 12: Distribution and Testimonials	121

CHAPTER 13: Timeline of the Literacy Project	129
CHAPTER 14: Demographics of the Literacy Project	139
CHAPTER 15: The Effects of Literacy Project on Sociocultural and Religious Attitudes	145
CHAPTER 16: Other Dynamics and Effects of the Literacy Study	151
CHAPTER 17: Analysis of Distribution and Supervision	161
CHAPTER 18: The Impact of the Literacy Program on Local Churches	167
CHAPTER 19: Contextualizing the Literacy Project	173
CHAPTER 20: Conclusion	199
References Cited	201

Preface

The study analyzed contextual influences on the development of a literacy program in Bangladesh that need to be considered for effective adaptation of the program in other cultural contexts.

Baseline research done in 1990 and experiments conducted during the development of the materials from 1991-1997 showed that only ten percent of the population could read the *New Reader Portions* from Bangladesh Bible Society. To address this challenge among new readers, new Scripture-focused audio products and primers were devised and implemented. The result was that thirty to forty percent could read the *New Readers' Portions* after using these new materials.

In April 2000, another extensive survey was conducted in six different districts of Bangladesh (Mymensingh, Gopalganj, Rajshahi, Bogra, Dinajpur, and Nilphamari) with 299 members of the literacy groups. This survey was conducted using a standard questionnaire. The ongoing effects of this literacy program continue to show thirty to forty percent being able to read.

Foreword

I am exceptionally pleased to offer this brief foreword to Teresa Chai's book, *Literacy and the Bible in Bangladesh*. She has been a dear friend and colleague for nearly seven years at the Asia Pacific Theological Seminary in Baguio City, Philippines, which is publishing this book as part of their APTS Press Monograph Series.

This book reflects the author's work over eight years as a missionary in Bangladesh, where she was involved with the United Bible Society and the Bangladesh Bible Society, then the Bangladesh Lutheran Church-Danish Mission and the Bangladesh Lutheran Church, despite the fact that Tess herself was a Pentecostal, in teaching literacy to the Bangladeshi people. The methods Tess advocates here were based on her actual fieldwork during her years there.

Sadly, Tess did not live to see the publication of her work. On Sunday morning, March 8, 2020, as this book was going to press, Tess went to be with the Lord she so loved, following a nine-month battle with pancreatic cancer.

From her entrance into the Bible College of Malaysia at the age of 20 until her passing at the age of 57, Tess dedicated her life to the Lord in full-time ministry. Following graduation, Teresa worked nationally and internationally with Asian Outreach Malaysia, including mission trips to Sarawak, East Malaysia, Singapore, Thailand, Indonesia, and the Philippines. She was ordained with the Assemblies of God and also served as an adjunct faculty member at her alma mater. She has also enjoyed ministry to children, youth, and adults.

In 1991, she completed a Masters in Arts in Cross-Cultural Studies at Fuller Theological Seminary, School of World Mission. One of her writing projects, "Towards Innovations in Non-Print Scripture for

Literacy Training," became the basis for work and research in Bangladesh from 1991 to 1999.

The eight years in Bangladesh, partially under the United Bible Societies and seconded to Bangladesh Bible Society, involved research and development of literacy such as audio and written Scriptures. Teresa also worked for Bangladesh Lutheran Mission–Danish (closely associated with the Bangladesh Lutheran Church). The literacy groups under the mission and church became the initial literacy test groups.

After completing her time in Bangladesh, she returned to Fuller to complete her PhD and this book is the published version of her dissertation. Then, she served for several years at the Alpha and Omega Bible College in Kuala Lumpur, Malaysia, first as the academic dean and later president, before moving to her final assignment at the Asia Pacific Theological Seminary (APTS) in Baguio City, Philippines, in May 2013, where she served as a faculty member and later, academic dean.

As one of her colleagues at APTS, I can say without fear of contradiction that she was deeply loved and is dearly missed, but we thank God for a life well lived.

Dave Johnson, DMiss
Managing Editor, *Asian Journal of Pentecostal Studies*
Asia Pacific Theological Seminary

Dedication

To my American parents,
Carl and Donna Schneider,
who have been there for me in countless ways

Acknowledgments

First and foremost, I want to express my deepfelt appreciation to the late Viggo B. Søgaard, who was a consultant with the United Bible Societies Communication and Media department and the Professor of Communication in the School of World Mission in Fuller Seminary. He has been my mentor and friend through his guidance and encouragement. He invested himself in my spiritual and academic development. I count it a great privilege and honor to have been mentored by him.

I also want to thank those who have taken time to guide me in this journey. I am grateful for invaluable insights from Elizabeth Sue Brewster on literacy, language, and culture and for Charles H. Kraft on anthropology and contextualization. A word of thanks to Julian Sundersingh, a consultant with the United Bible Societies. I truly appreciate the comments and input from Helen H. Yim-Choi, who graciously took time to read and comment on the initial manuscript. I am grateful to James Jennings and the late Robert Rice for their advice and input as well.

Research and experimentation for this literacy program would not have been possible without the help and sponsorship of these organizations: United Bible Societies, Asia Pacific Regional office, Bangladesh Bible Society, Danish Mission Denmark, Bangladesh Lutheran Mission–Danish, Bangladesh Lutheran Church, and all other participating churches. My special thanks to the former Executive General Secretary of the Bangladesh Bible Society, James Halder, and Richmond Joydhor, the former Media Officer, and the literacy supervisors who helped in the field survey research. I also want to thank Stephen Baroi, the retired Country Director of Bangladesh

Lutheran Mission–Danish for making many of the arrangements when I went up north to visit the literacy groups. Likewise, my appreciation goes to the late Moses Muthusamy, the Malaysian missionary church advisor of the Bangladesh Lutheran Church, who was a kind host when I stayed in Birganj, and to the members of the church Synod for their cooperation and support.

Several people helped me with editorial work. I want to thank Bee Bee Tan, a Bible college classmate, who did the preliminary editing of my writing via the internet from Malaysia. My "American mother" Donna Schneider spent many hours reading and re-reading my work adding her editorial suggestions—thanks, Mom. Garrett Anderson took me through the last stages of editing and formatting. A special "thank you" to Laura Hollister for her excellent professional work as Research Librarian, making sure that every "jot and tittle" was in place. For recent edits I want to thank Rosemarie Kowalski, who gave very helpful suggestions for changes. Thanks also to Frank McNelis for doing the copyediting. I am also grateful to Elizabeth Glanville, the former Doctoral Program Advisor, who was always so encouraging and kind to me. Many family members and friends were my prayer supporters, including my sister Mary Ann Chai, and friends Siew Pik Lim and Katie Price-Foster.

Finally, all glory, honor and thanks to God, my Heavenly Father, for his blessings, strength, guidance, and grace. He blessed me beyond measure, gave me new strength when I felt like giving up, guided me through the maze of information, and granted me grace when I needed it.

List of Tables

TABLE 1:	Changes in UNESCO Definitions of Being Literate	9
TABLE 2:	Comparison of Selected Regional Literacy Rates (2016)	12
TABLE 3:	Adult Literacy Rates in Selected South Asian Countries (2015-2016)	13
TABLE 4:	Illiteracy Rates by Population in Bangladesh Over a Thirty-five Year Period (1981-2015)	14
TABLE 5:	Materials Summary of *Shukhbor*	99
TABLE 6:	Materials Summary of *Muktir Path*	100
TABLE 7:	Format Plan for *Shukhobor* 3 Product 1, Side A	106
TABLE 8:	Characterization of Nagen and Ravi	107
TABLE 9:	Color Coding Scheme for the Entire Literacy Products	111
TABLE 10:	Summary of Individual and Group Use	114
TABLE 11:	Facilitators' Responsibilities	116
TABLE 12:	Budget Items Per Test Period	122
TABLE 13:	Summary of Reading and Comprehension Results	132
TABLE 14:	Research Objectives	135
TABLE 15:	Research Design	137
TABLE 16:	Sampling Plan	137
TABLE 17:	Summary of Demographic Information	143
TABLE 18:	Reading Abilities of Respondents	154
TABLE 19:	Comprehension Abilities of Respondents	154
TABLE 20:	Cross-Tabulations of Reading *Shukhobor* 1 with New Readers	156
TABLE 21:	Cross-Tabulation of Reading *Shukhobor* 2 with New Readers	156
TABLE 22:	Cross-Tabulation of Reading NRP with New Readers	157
TABLE 23:	Cross-Tabulation of Reading Newspaper Headline with New Readers	158
TABLE 24:	Cross Tabulation of Writing and Doing Math with New Readers	158
TABLE 25:	Other Uses of the Literacy Materials	162
TABLE 26:	Churches Involved in the Literacy Program	167

List of Figures

FIGURE 1	Process of Translation	77
FIGURE 2	Source, Mearning, and Receptor Model of Communication	78
FIGURE 3	Translation Process	81
FIGURE 4	Comprehensive Communication Process	87
FIGURE 5	Bengali Combined Letters	102
FIGURE 6	Program Management System	118
FIGURE 7	Religions of the Respondents by Percentage	140
FIGURE 8	Educational Levels of the Respondents by Percentage	142
FIGURE 9	Reasons Respondents Wanted to Learn by Percentage	146
FIGURE 10	Respondents' Knowledge About Christianity	148
FIGURE 11	Knowledge of "Good Stories" Before the Class Began	149
FIGURE 12	Respondents' Enjoyment of the Class	151
FIGURE 13	Respondents' Level of Learning From Classes	152

List of Abbreviations

ABWE	Association of Baptist for World Evangelization Baptist for World Evangelization
AIDS	Acquired Immune Deficiency Syndrome
AL	Awami League
ALP	Adult Literacy Program
BARD	Bangladesh Academy for Rural Development
BBS	Bangladesh Bible Society
BLC	Bangladesh Lutheran Church
BLM	Bangladesh Lutheran Mission
BLM-D	Bangladesh Lutheran Mission—Danish
BNELC	Bangladesh Northern Evangelical Lutheran Church
BNP	Bangladesh National Party
BRAC	Bangladesh Rural Advancement Committee
BSA	Bible Society of Australia
B. Th.	Bachelor of Theology
BTV	Bangladesh Television
CCDB	Christian Commission for Development in Bangladesh
CCTB	College of Christian Theology Bangladesh
DMCDO	Danish Missionary Council Development Office
	Denom. Denominational
DSM	Danish Santal Mission
ETV	Ekushey Television
FC	Field Coordinator
FIVDB	Friends in Village Development Bangladesh
FS	Field Supervisor
ILI	International Literacy Institute
LEI	Literacy Evangelism International
LWF	Lutheran World Federation
NGO	Non-Government Organization
NIV	New International Version

NRP	New Readers' Portions
RSC	Regional Service Center
SDA	Seventh Day Adventist
SIL	Summer Institute of Linguistics
UBS	United Bible Societies
UN	United Nations
UNICEF	United Nations International Children's Educational Fund
UNESCO	United Nations Educational Scientific and Cultural Organization

Definition of Phrases

1. Appropriate media is preferred as opposed to just general media. In developing countries, finances and technology limit resources. This media should be accessible in rural and urban settings.
2. Bangladesh is the country of context. Its language is Bangla or Bengali. Bengali or Bangladeshi is a term used for a citizen of Bangladesh. The word "Bangladeshi" is also used to imply ownership.
3. Culture circle: a discussion group in which educators and learners engage in dialogue about the reasons for their existential situation. The peer group provides the theoretical context for reflection and for transforming interpretations of reality from mere opinion to a more critical knowledge.
4. Encoding: utilizing the mind to put the message into a coded system.
5. Decoding: reversing the encoding process and turning the code back into a message.
6. Innovation in literacy training: the adaptation of established ways of using media.
7. Media-based: communication in which media is the main form.
8. Media literacy: the process of understanding and using the mass media.
9. Multimedia: combined media, such as sound, video, text, or images.
10. A multimedia approach: a communication process taking place on different levels and with more than one medium.
11. Primers: printed materials of Scriptural passages and writing exercises used in the teaching and learning process of the program.
12. Scripture-focused: literacy materials that primarily use biblical stories and passages in the audio products and primers

CHAPTER 1

Introduction

A common Bengali greeting is *"Apni kemon achen?"* This translates to *"How are You?"* Bengali is a language spoken by over 130 million people in Bangladesh, India and other parts of the world where Bengali speakers have migrated. Religion in Bangladesh breaks down to eighty-seven percent Muslim, ten percent Hindu, two percent Buddhist, with Christianity and indigenous tribal religions making up the remaining one percent. Official literacy statistics indicate that approximately seventy percent of Bangladeshis are able to read a sentence and sign their names in their own language with varying levels of skills. This should have serious implications for the national churches in Bangladesh in at least two ways. The Church needs to find creative ways to present the gospel and to instruct church members in the Word of God. Literacy programs could be seen as a means of helping people in the community not only in literacy training but also as outreach to them.

Bangladesh's population, the eighth largest in the world, contains the poorest of the poor. There is relatively little industry, and most people live at a subsistence level in rural areas. The political system is unstable. Adding to the nation's woes are natural disasters, such as tropical storms whipping in from the Bay of Bengal and devastating the country.

Despite its problems, Bangladesh is a land of miracles and heroic accomplishments. Using traditional methods, farmers manage to produce enough food to maintain one of the densest concentrations of rural people in the world. The Bangladeshis have liberated themselves twice—from the British and from the Pakistanis. The Bangla language has a distinguished history in literature and remains one of the most dynamic forces in South Asian arts and humanities. This is the country in which a unique literacy program was developed.

Personal Background

I have a vested interest in this literacy program as a Christian, Malaysian-Chinese woman who was working in Bangladesh for eight years from October 1991 to December 1999. For the first two and a half years, I served with the United Bible Societies (UBS) as a research assistant to Viggo Søgaard. For the remaining years, I worked for Bangladesh Lutheran Mission – Danish (BLM-D), which is related to the Bangladesh Lutheran Church (BLC). I also continued to have direct involvement and responsibilities in the literacy program in cooperation with Bangladesh Bible Society (BBS).

Even prior to working for UBS, as part of my masters program at Fuller School of World Mission, I did a baseline research study on the BLM-D literacy program. I also studied whether new readers could read the New Readers' Portions (NRP), which are the materials produced by UBS. My writing project developed a proposal for an alternative approach, utilizing new innovations that used Scriptures in literacy training. After graduating from Fuller in 1991, I returned to implement these strategies within BBS and BLM-D. This resulted in a comprehensive literacy program with Scripture-focused and media-based audio products and literacy primers developed for literacy training. All of these are still being used by churches in Bangladesh. Furthermore, other national Bible Societies have requested to adapt the program in order to meet the literacy needs in their countries. When I was at the Lausanne meeting in Cape Town, South Africa, 2010, I saw a video presentation that featured this literacy program in Bangladesh. It warmed my heart that God was still using this program, presenting the Good News.

Precedent Research

Since I built on the precedent research done during my masters program as well as the extensive research conducted during the development of the materials, it will be appropriate for me to briefly describe what has been already done. I designed research procedures to get baseline data on BLM-D's literacy program and also to evaluate whether the Bible Society's NRPs could be read by new readers. The survey research, done within the span of seven weeks, was conducted with a random sample of one hundred past students from two different districts with ten persons from each village. During this time, Bangladesh was in great political turmoil, as the former Prime Minister of the country, Hussain Mohammed Ershad, was being ousted by the opposition parties. Despite strikes and curfew periods I was able to conduct the research.

The data revealed the tensions of ideals and realities that the respondents faced. On the one hand, they valued literacy while, on the other, they faced the stark reality of their lack of literacy skills. Seventy percent responded that reading, writing, and counting are important skills in daily life. Yet, of the sample, only ten percent were functionally literate, which illustrates the vast gap between perceived value of literacy and the practice of it. The research identified seven factors that were affecting the effectiveness of a literacy program: 1) group dynamics, 2) increase of social status as people sought the help of those who could read, 3) encouragement from family and friends, 4) curriculum being practical in content, easy to follow, and understandable, 5) availability of local teachers, 6) length and frequency of a program and 7) follow-up after completion. There was also an interest in the inclusion of an audio component that contained stories from the Bible. These issues would need to be taken seriously in the development of a new program.

Experimentation of a Scripture-Focused and Media-Based Literacy Program

I proposed that materials be made for those who had gone through a basic literacy course, not for those at zero-level literacy. The Scripture-focused and media-based literacy program developed is one that is self-contained; that is, the materials can be used independently by new readers, whether as individuals or as a group, without a literacy teacher. This is possible as the audio products and the primers are incorporated as a teaching guide. Characters on the audio products play students and a storyteller who tells or reads the Scriptures. Interspersed are appropriate dramas or songs based on the scriptural text or a main need-oriented theme to keep the listener interested. Primers are used for reading and writing exercises.

Two tracks for this program were developed. One track, for general village use, incorporates need-oriented themes suitable for new readers and uses portions of Scripture that are related to the theme. The second track is for church leaders and covers the life of Christ, Old Testament characters, selected New Testament readings, and Christian topics, such as faith. All these materials were pre-tested and revised at least ten times before a final product was released for extensive field tests. The result now is the availability of three sets of four audio products and primers for track one and twenty-two audio products for track two.

These materials were used with groups under BLC and BLM-D as an experiment of the Scripture-focused and media-based literacy program for two years. Necessary support materials such as audio devices and batteries to run them were supplied. In each literacy center there were two groups, one of men and the other of women. They shared the materials provided except for the primers. People were appointed to handle the distribution and administration of the materials and program. Participants' progress was monitored by taking attendance and by testing, which was administered at the end of each set.

This experimentation yielded some positive results evident in the testing period that would deem this program useful for other countries with a similar challenge of low literacy. Therefore, deriving guidelines for adapting this program is expedient.

Purpose of the Study

The purpose of this study is to analyze contextual elements of a Scripture-focused and media-based adult literacy program developed in Bangladesh in order to develop guidelines for cross-cultural adaptation of the program.

Significance of the Study

This study is significant to me personally because I hope to see this program widely used in other developing countries. I believe that communication principles can significantly assist in making the program adaptable. UBS will find this study significant, as will other national Bible Societies in countries with low literacy that are keen to consider developing materials using Scripture in literacy training. The BLC and BLM-D, other national churches, and mission organizations in Bangladesh that have literacy programs will be eager to know if the program has helped the national churches especially in propagating the gospel, developing leadership, and becoming self-supporting. Literacy organizations such as Literacy Evangelism International (LEI) and Summer Institute of Linguistics (SIL) will be interested in this study since it relates to their ministry.

The long-term missiological significance of this study is to suggest adaptation guidelines for using these Scripture-focused and media-based literacy materials in other countries that want to use them. It is estimated that seventeen percent of the world's people are illiterate (Roser and Ortiz-Ospina 2018:n.p.).

Problem Statement

The problem addressed in this study is the identification of the contextual influences on the development of a literacy program in Bangladesh that should be adapted in order for the program to be effective in another cultural context.

Research Questions

The study will seek to answer the following questions:

1. What are the contextual factors that have influenced the development and results of this Scripture-focused and media-based literacy program in Bangladesh?

2. What are the current issues facing adult literacy programs in developing countries that will need to be considered for future approaches?

3. What are the media factors that have influenced the media-based literacy program's effectiveness?

4. What are the contextual factors that need to be considered for the adaptation of this Scripture-focused and media-based literacy program to other contexts?

Delimitations

This study will not include all types of media. It will focus on audio products and literacy primers as the main form of media-mix. The main denominational context of the study is the national Bengali Lutheran Church. Therefore, the study will not include all denominations. It will not cover all literacy programs in Bangladesh, only the specific one developed for the United Bible Societies and the Bangladesh Lutheran Mission – Danish.

Assumptions

Some major assumptions of this study are:

1. Reading will empower poverty-stricken people to have access to information they need.

2. The United Bible Societies wanted to include a variety of media in their ministry for effective Scripture communication.

3. Communication principles can assist in the adaptation of a program from one context to another context, even though some factors are different.

4. This Scripture-focused and media-based adult literacy program will be on the cutting edge in bringing the gift of functional literacy to the people who need it.

CHAPTER 2

The Challenge of Illiteracy

Illiteracy poses a great challenge. "774 million people aged 15 and older are illiterate, an infographic from UNESCO details. 52 percent live in south and west Asia and 22 percent in sub-Saharan Africa" (Kristina C.: 2013).

Beyond that, many people are functionally non-literate (unable to read and write a simple message in any language). Yet the Bible is usually in print: most Christian ministries use printed materials to communicate with their target audience. How can a person know what is written if he or she could not read? Christian radio ministries depended on written feedback from listeners. How can a person respond to a radio show in the required written form if he or she could not write? Christian literacy programs attempt to bridge this gap in teaching literacy skills.

Defining Literacy

Literacy means different things to different people in different contexts. Defining "literate" can be a daunting task. A psychologist, a pedagogical educator, or a policy writer for the government may have his or her own definition. However, it is important to have a working definition as a backdrop.

The Summer Institute of Linguistics glossary of terms states, "Literacy is the quality or state of being able to read and write" (SIL International—LinguaLinks Library 4.0:2000). Harbans S. Bhola, former professor at the Indiana University, gives the following expanded understanding of literacy:

Literacy is not merely a skill, that is, the skill of reading and writing. It is a powerful potential—a quality with many uses—given to individual men and women, boys and girls who become literate. Literacy makes it possible for individuals to use their minds in new and different ways. It is the ability to find and use new information that gives them a new sense of freedom. Literacy is a social process. It brings the literate person new respect and social status. This happens even though other changes in their lives take more time. Literacy can and does bring development to societies. (1994:17-18)

The 1992 and 2003 National Assessments of Adult Literacy in the United States of America provide the following definition: "using printed and written information to function in society, to achieve one's goals, and to develop one's knowledge and potential" (National Center for Education Statistics n.d.:n.p.). This definition goes beyond simply decoding and comprehending text to include a broad range of information-processing skills that an adult uses in accomplishing the range of tasks associated with work, home, and community contexts.

Policy-making communities such as the United States Congress have incorporated a similar definition into the National Literacy Act of 1991. They defined literacy as "an individual's ability to read, write, and speak English and compute and solve problems at levels of proficiency necessary to function on the job and in society, to achieve one's goals, and to develop one's knowledge and potential" (National Center for Education Statistics n.d.:n.p.).

In general, literacy can be defined in a functional way. A person's skills of reading and writing may influence his or her ability to access and process information in the thinking processes, development as a person, cope with life's problems, and achieve goals.

Progressive Definitions of Literacy

Definitions of literacy have evolved over time. In the Bangla language of Bangladesh, the word "literacy" refers to "signature." Each census of literacy in Bangladesh has used a different definition of a literate person. This means the actual changes in literacy rates are not known due to lack of consistency in definitions. This causes great confusion and makes comparisons impossible.

UNESCO has been instrumental in creating international definitions of literacy. In any census before 1951, a person was counted as literate who said he or she could sign his or her name (Khan 1979:1). For a new census in 1951, UNESCO changed their definition to "those who could read clear printing in any language" (Jennings 1990:24). There was no reference to writing. A problem in this earlier definition was that, while some Muslims in Bangladesh read the Quran in Arabic, they could not understand it.

In 1961, another census was taken. UNESCO added to the definition of literacy that reading must be with understanding. In 1974, the definition expanded to include the ability of a person to write his or her name, words, and complete sentences. By 1981, the standard was raised to include the ability to write a letter to a family member or a friend. (This is a useful article on the situation in 2011: https://bdeduarticle.com/literacy-and-adult-education-in-bangladesh-concept-trends-status-and-the-future/)

TABLE 1: CHANGES IN UNESCO DEFINITIONS OF BEING LITERATE

Year	pre-1951	1951	1961	1974	1981
Definitions of being literate	Able to sign one's name	Reading with or without understanding	Reading with understanding	Reading with understanding, writing one's name, writing words and complete sentences	Reading with understanding, writing one's name, writing words and complete sentences, including a letter to a family member or friend

Table 1 summarizes these definitions of literacy over the years for Bangladesh. Those counted as literate before 1951 included those who could sign their names but who might not actually read or write. Later, more reliable, statistics are not uniform in measuring and comparing literacy rates.

This study was mainly concerned with adult literacy. The term "adult" has no uniform definition, but adults learn differently from children. Adults have more life experience and knowledge on which to build. They may also have different motivations for wanting to learn. This was made clear in the 1962 UNESCO definition of literacy:

> A person is literate when he [or she] has acquired the essential knowledge and skills which enable him [or her] to engage in all those activities in which literacy is required for effective functioning in his [or her] group and community, and whose attainments in reading, writing and arithmetic make it possible for [or her] to continue to use these skills towards his [or her] own and the community's development. (Harman 1970:227)

This definition does not emphasize reading, writing, and counting, but rather that these skills are a means to an end. The goal is to improve oneself and contribute to the development of one's community.

In summary, literacy has traditionally been defined as the ability to read, write, and comprehend texts. Early definitions did not include what it means to be functionally literate, but later definitions point to functional literacy when one possesses the skills necessary for the fulfillment of self-determined objectives. These objectives are related to his or her family, community, social and religious circles, jobs, or any other associations of choice. A literate person can obtain wanted or needed information, to be used for his or her and others' well-being. He or she should be able to read and write adequately to solve problems encountered in daily life (Price and Karr 1985:7-8).

Adult Illiteracy Rates

The adult literacy rate is defined as the percentage of the population aged fifteen years and over who can read with understanding and write a short simple statement about his or her daily life. Adult literacy rates usually show how well primary education and literacy programs have imparted basic literacy skills, enabled an adult to apply such skills in daily life, and taught them to keep learning and communicating using the written word. Literacy represents a potential for further intellectual growth and contribution to the economic-sociocultural development of society. In contrast, illiteracy rates indicate the extent of need for policies and efforts in organizing adult literacy programs and quality primary education.

World Illiteracy Rates

UNESCO has relied almost entirely on its member countries to provide data for worldwide statistical comparisons. These countries typically depend on national census information, which most often determines literacy ability by self-stated years of primary schooling or self-assessment questionnaires. These measures are likely to be unreliable indicators of literacy ability, but they are the only ones available. However, some changes are happening. Systematic national or regional surveys that actually measure literacy skills have been instituted in a few industrialized countries.

Recent UNESCO statistics show that world illiteracy rates dropped during the 1980s and 1990s due to increased primary school enrollments. Yet, this data also indicates that the actual numbers of non-literates have remained generally constant due to population growth. Optimistically, programs for achieving universal primary schooling and adult literacy could lead to a drop towards a zero illiteracy rate by 2025. These hopeful views seem to be shared by few specialists in the field, but occasionally they are put forward by policy makers to present the best face possible on literacy developments. A more realistic view indicates that data on world literacy rates is misleading and underestimates the nature and scope of literacy problems. Furthermore, neither increases in primary school nor adult literacy programs have effectively reduced illiteracy rates.

General views of literacy rates mask large inequalities. Literacy rates may be high in urban areas while illiteracy is high in rural communities, among girls and women, and, perhaps most importantly for the future, among marginalized, minority, and indigenous groups. In most developing and many industrialized countries there are also severe educational inefficiencies, making universal primary schooling and increased adult literacy hard to achieve. We can also note that illiteracy rates vary significantly in different areas of the world. UNESCO reports that eighty percent of the world is literate, but, as seen in Table 2, there are significant variations in selected areas. From Table 2, literacy rates in Sub-Saharan Africa and Southern Asia are higher than in other regions.

TABLE 2: COMPARISON OF SELECTED REGIONAL LITERACY RATES (2016)

UNESCO Region	Adult Literacy Rate by Percentage		
	Total	Male	Female
Sub-Saharan Africa	39.1	30.0	45.8
Southern Asia	47.1	34.1	59.0
Latin America and the Caribbean	18.9	16.2	21.1
Eastern and South-Eastern Asia	14.5	7.4	20.5
Central Asia	1.1	0.6	1.4

Latin America and the Caribbean, Eastern and South-Eastern Asia have less that twenty-one percent literacy. The illiteracy rates for Central Asia countries show the urgency and magnitude of the task at hand. Bangladesh, Nepal, Pakistan, and India face the challenge of raising their literacy rates as well (see Table 3. India is not in this list.) However, the twenty-five countries with the lowest literacy rates are South Sudan to Togo (The World Factbook 2018:n.p).

TABLE 3: ADULT LITERACY RATES IN SELECTED SOUTH ASIAN COUNTRIES (2015-2016)

Country	Adult Literacy Rate by Percentage		
	Total	Male	Female
Bangladesh	72.8	75.6	69.9
Nepal	63.9	76.4	53.1
Pakistan	57.9	69.5	45.8
India	71.2	81.3	60.6
Iran	79.7	85.7	73.7
Sri Lanka	92.6	93.6	91.7
Maldives	99.3	99.8	98.8

Illiteracy Rate in Bangladesh

As noted above, there have been inconsistent definitions of being literate and times without an actual reading or writing evaluation. Early data counted people as literate if they were able to sign their names, according to the Bengali understanding of being literate. Table 4 should, therefore, be interpreted for literacy trends but not as an exact account of the literacy rate, which is at a low rise.

Generally speaking, people have higher literacy rates in urban settings than those in rural areas. Literacy rates among men are higher than among women. Table 4 shows illiteracy rates over a thirty-five year period (The World Factbook 2018:n.p.). A major change between 1981 and 1999 could be due to the mandatory ruling to send children to school, which caused a spike in the literacy rate between those years (Jennings 1990:21). It has slowed down again although the ministry of education claimed in 2015 that literacy rate has risen to seventy percent (Staff correspondent bdnews 24:2015).

TABLE 4: ILLITERACY RATES BY POPULATION IN BANGLADESH OVER A THIRTY-FIVE-YEAR PERIOD (1981-2015)

Year	1981	1991	2001	2014	2015
Entire Country	32,583,020	40,740,776	44,544,152	43,915,940	43,738,120
Change		25.0%	9.34%	-1.41%	-0.40%
Population					160,995,642

Struggles of a Non-Literate

The state of being literate is not the same as being intelligent; a person who cannot read and write may be intelligent. However, a person who cannot read or write faces serious disadvantages. An illiterate person may sign away his or her property to unscrupulous or dishonest people who take advantage of other people's weaknesses. Non-literates are unable to access information in print—for instance, instruction labels on medicine boxes or bottles. Those who cannot read may die because they take the wrong medicine or dosage.

Despite the benefits of reading and writing, people often lack interest in literacy classes. They may doubt that being literate will be useful. A "luxury" activity such as literacy classes may be viewed as a waste of time; time is better spent in finding ways to increase income and food. Other practical considerations include "physical health, gender, number of small children, parental education, stability of home life, and opportunities to practice literacy outside the classroom" (Abadzi 1994:15). In countries where poverty is a day-to-day struggle, it is difficult to see the need for individual literacy, and even less so for a female. True ownership of the benefits of literacy requires overcoming such mindsets.

Feminization of Illiteracy

The illiteracy rate is higher among women than men in developing countries. According to the UNESCO World Education Report, almost one out of five persons cannot read. Women account for 65 percent of the world's non-literate population. This report adds that in 2000, women's illiteracy rate in Asia stood at 32 percent, in Africa 31 percent, and in the Arab States 28 percent. In 2001 in Nepal, 93 percent of women over thirty could not read (Rice 2001: Interview). Most illiterate women in developing countries are concentrated in rural and marginal urban areas, where social economic inequalities are more evident. In recent years, there has been a slight increase in girls' school enrollment. In Bangladesh, an incentive program gives stipends and wheat to families who send their girls to school. Frank Laubach said, "When we educate a woman we educate a whole household" (Laubach 1950:17). Education of females is important, but as yet it is a neglected issue.

In one instance, twenty women from a rural village in Bangladesh are sitting in a literacy class. Wives of landless day-laborers, they bring their small children with them. Theirs is a hand-to-mouth existence. They were shown a picture of a woman dressed much like themselves in a torn and tattered *saree* with five children sitting with her. These women in this class all look as starved as the woman in the picture. The caption on this poster, written in Bangla, was "*Khedah Lage,*" which means "Hunger." These women may not have been able to read the words but they did understand the picture. They could picture themselves as the starving woman and her children because in their village they have experienced floods and cyclones, followed by the lack of food. As they learned how to read this word "hunger," they already knew the reality of its meaning. This group developed to be more than a literacy class; later, these women formed a savings group and an income-generating weaving project. They were motivated to learn and use their literacy skills as a means to an end. In five years, they achieved a seventh-grade reading level. Unfortunately, not all situations have had such a positive outcome.

Another obstacle to achieving literacy is religion. Some religions limit a woman's role to the domestic domain, which can constrain her participation in adult literacy classes. However, expert educators and researchers agree that the main reason for women's lack of participation in educational activities is poverty. The feminization of illiteracy is closely related to the feminization of poverty. Women risk becoming poor because of family rupture, divorce or separation, husband migration, and the undermining of women's roles in society. Without skills or education, women are in a vulnerable position (Ballara 1999:1-3). Girls have difficulties attending formal schools, and adult women in extreme poverty, with unfulfilled basic needs, cannot participate in literacy programs.

In most homes with low incomes, women play reproductive and economic roles. Educational activities are relegated to a secondary place due to a lack of time. Often, women may not attend literacy or education activities because of their husbands' opposition. Children are an important part of the labor force, so they are not sent to school.

In certain societies, women and children are treated with less importance than men. At an early age, they have less access to formal education and, in many cases, to food and health care. Discrimination starts in early childhood and tends to continue throughout their lives.

UNESCO highlights the fact that women's and children's illiteracy are due to their subordinate situation. Male family members may be afraid of a more egalitarian position of women and children in the family as a result of female achievements gained through education. Literacy and education contribute to the development of critical thoughts and can jeopardize the expected roles imposed on women by society. This poses a risk and threat for those who benefit from women's subordinate position. Those who feel threatened may use various means and present obstacles in order to hinder women, boys, and girls from participating in education (Ballara 1999:4-9).

We see a vast contrast between the treatment of women by some men and the biblical accounts of how Jesus treated women. In New Testament times women were vulnerable. Jesus showed by example that he respected women's needs and did not despise them. He saw them as persons made in the image of God, speaking and listening to them. The Lord esteemed women who were shunned or despised by the society in that age. One example is the Samaritan woman at the well who later became an evangelist among her own people (John 4:1-42). The woman who poured perfume on Jesus' feet was commended for her act (Mark 14:1-9). Jesus noticed the widow who gave an offering, as more worthy than all the offerings of the wealthy combined (Mark 12:41-44). Christ's demonstrations of the value of women as human beings should be imitated. In the context of this study, this includes the right for women to learn how to read and write.

Determinants of Adult Literacy Acquisition

A number of other factors may determine whether a person will acquire functional literacy. Some lie within an individual. Most research tends to diagnose external factors like teaching methods, teacher training, time availability of the poor, and organizational breakdowns. These are easier to measure than internal motivational factors. But there is also a need also to focus on the latter.

Some assumptions underlie literacy acquisition. Foremost is the assumption of a student's internal motivation to become literate. Second, there must be a body of literature available for them to read. Third, the communication skills of reading and writing parallel those in listening and speaking, with the assumption that writing skill reinforces reading skill. A final assumption is that reading encompasses all aspects of language.

Attitudes and Beliefs as a Determining Factor

Attitudes and beliefs play an important role in literacy acquisition. In a family that is not literate, there may be no encouragement to learn to read. Becoming literate may even be forbidden. Sociologists Kahneman and Miller propose the "norm theory" that suggests "people are accustomed to the presence of certain factors in their lives, which they regard as normal (these may include illiteracy and sanitation)" (Abadzi 1994:15). The struggle is that those who cannot read and write see being unable to read and write as a normal state, while literacy workers regard being literate as normal. Another hindrance may be a belief that one is too old to learn or that it would upset the balance in the culture if too many women can read and write.

Motivation as a Determining Factor

The desire to become literate is the single most important factor in acquiring literacy. It is a more important motivation than the teaching method, the quality of teaching, the capability of the teacher, or even the adequacy of the writing system of the language. However, motivation as a lead determining factor does not undermine the role of other factors.

Good teaching methods encourage students to progress faster and thereby boost their motivation. A good teacher and an adequate writing system foster existing motivation, but a poor method, teacher, or orthography can kill motivation that is not intense. Gudschinsky observed that much of the literature on functional literacy discusses the motivation for learning and the use of literacy skills to the exclusion of concern with literacy methods. However, adequate pedagogy requires attention to the mechanics of literacy teaching (1973:2). Harmon stated that "while initial motivation relies upon variations of persuasion, continuing motivation derives from the program itself—its substance and method" (1970:256).

During the survey done in Bangladesh, the following reasons were given for why new readers were motivated to learn:

- Read the Bible
- Read and write letters to relatives
- Help children with schoolwork
- Get further education
- Teach others
- Get a job or find a better one
- For social position in the community
- Know one's rights and responsibilities in society
- Participate in social and political activities
- No longer be cheated by others
- Improve living conditions for oneself and others
- Marry a more educated person and not pay a high dowry, in the case of women (Chai 2000:21).

Frequently, the motivation to become literate stems from a desire to read religious literature. Even for cultures in which religion is not a primary motivator, it may have been a primary motivating factor in their history. In the seventeenth and eighteenth centuries, in the British colonies which became the United States, the primary motivation for literacy was to read the Bible and other religious literature. Primers were full of quotations from the Bible and the catechism; the religious instructional content reflected the main interest of the community.

The desire to get a job, gain prestige, make material gains, or instigate social and political reform may provide motivation. However, without accompanying literature that is considered relevant, motivation is likely to diminish before full literacy is attained. This issue has not always been given attention by literacy programs. At times, long-term goals of new readers are compromised by immediate constraints like lack of time to attend classes, limited attention spans, and no grasp of the advantage of literacy.

Women often face additional barriers of heavy workloads in the family. Male family members may oppose women's learning, fearing that the women will know more than they do. Women who memorize certain facts and ask others for help may convince themselves that literacy is not needed.

Illiteracy traps women in a cycle of poverty and limited options for economic improvement. Their children are sentenced to chronic poverty by limited educational and training opportunities. Frequently the only "skill" a poor woman has is prostitution as a means for daily bread and support for her children. The soil is fertile for an epidemic of AIDS. Lack of female literacy is also closely associated with increased infant and child mortality and illness (Rice 2002:31).

Students dropping out of classes were a problem. A typical adult literacy class gave control to a teacher. A central agency dictated materials to be learned, which may or may not be what the learners wanted or needed. Dropping out was one escape from such a directive environment, but a participant-centered approach could minimize this attrition.

Lack of Appropriate Reading Material

A successful literacy program keeps new readers literate after basic courses are completed. According to B. Dumont, "Post-literacy work can be defined as all those materials and structures which enable the newly literate adult to keep up, use and develop the knowledge he (or she) has acquired and the abilities generated in him through literacy teaching" (1979:146). Therefore, long-term plans of literacy programs should incorporate structures that continue to feed material to the newly literate.

The first task was to seek out what literature was available. In Bangladesh, the following were organizations that provided materials specifically for new readers. Friends in Village Development Bangladesh [FIVDB] produced a monthly newsletter (Good resource for writing for new literates. https://scholarworks.umass.edu/cgi/viewcontent.cgi?article=1002&context=cie_actionlearningmanual (accessed February 15, 2020)). The Bangladesh Bible Society had a Literacy Skill Development Project (http://biblesociety.org.bd/project/literacy-skill-development-project-for-the-underprivileged/(accessed February 15, 2020)). Jennings noted an ongoing need to put post-literacy reading materials in the hands of new readers (1990:222). New readers must also be encouraged toward a higher level of literacy.

Literacy materials should be motivational and address the real and felt needs listed above. These materials should build up self-esteem and self-confidence in users.

Lack of Emphasis on Primary Education

Another aspect of the lack of literacy is low attendance of children and youth in primary school. The basic right of children and youth to education is related to poverty and gender issues. Bangladesh is committed to the World Declaration of Education for All and its government has passed the Compulsory Primary Education Act of 1990. Programs such as Food for Education, free textbook distribution, and a stipend for girls for going to school encouraged parents to send their children to school.

In 1998 there were 45,000 primary schools and 170,000 teachers in Bangladesh, with about twenty to twenty five million children who are six to ten years old. Yet, fifteen percent of these children do not enter primary school and forty percent drop out before completion (The World Bank Group 1998:n.p.). In 2004, 1.5 million children of school going age were not in school (Uddin, World Bank 2014:n.p.). The most pressing reason why children cannot complete their studies is economic. Poverty-stricken families simply cannot afford sending their children to school.[1] (More primary education information, https://www.usaid.gov/bangladesh/education (accessed February 15, 2020)).

Another practical consideration is the structural organization of primary schools. A primary school must be nearby for a rural family. Primary schools should supply learning materials, have flexible school hours to accommodate daily and seasonal work, and hire committed teachers. Many schools in Bangladesh are in a terrible state of disrepair, with a shortage of outdoor activities and playgrounds, overcrowded classrooms, and non-working latrines and water supplies. Much of the curriculum is archaic and irrelevant to real life. Poor-quality textbooks contain many misprints and outdated information. They are not properly distributed, so many books end up on the black market. (See link on primary education in the paragraph above.)

The role of teachers is also important to the success of primary education. The teacher-student ratio is approximately 1:42. The global standard is 1:30 (http://annx.asianews.network/content/teacher-student-ratio-worsens-bangladesh-46376(accessed February 15, 2020)). Due to low salaries, teachers resort to private tuition classes with paying students, at the expense of not being a good teacher in their regular school job. In addition to sub-standard economic conditions, physical school facilities, and teachers (Gustavsson 1989:49-50).

In the macro perspective, communities and government must take ownership of the situation. Village school systems in Bangladesh have a school management committee. In many cases, these committees are not active in improving the situation for the children. For school systems to improve, the government must invest in better schools and teachers. Although education itself is free, student costs include examination fees, private tutoring, and other fees. These add up and make education too expensive for a poor family. It is no wonder that poor children do not have a chance at proper education (Gustavsson 1989:57-58). Not a lot has changed over the years for Bangladesh

---

[1] On the positive side, education begets education. But if parents of children are not educated themselves, they will not see any importance or value of education for their children but there are always exceptions, of course (Gustavsson 1990:49-130).

(Accessed February 15, 2020, https://www.studycountry.com/guide/BD-education.htm).

Challenge of Illiteracy

Illiteracy has serious implications for society and in the Church. Communication cannot be done only in written form. Statistics can lull us into thinking that the war against illiteracy has being won, yet the task ahead is still substantial.

The General Population

According to a United Nations report,

Countries that have been most successful in reducing poverty are those that emphasized universal primary education, primary health care and rural development. In some cases, as in China and Vietnam, levels of poverty were greatly reduced while per capita incomes were low because of the provision of education, health care and employment opportunities. Conversely, in countries where illiteracy remained high and public health care was poor, poverty reduction efforts were less successful (UNICEF 2000:n.p.).

With little or no emphasis on education, illiteracy impacts all aspects of society, including crime rates, employment opportunities, income levels, and repeating the cycle with children. The vicious web of poverty is therefore not broken for a society that is already hurting.

The Church

Education is accorded to the privileged. Globally, lack of education and illiteracy is widespread, with a wide disparity between affluent and poor countries. The places with the poorest people, the most oppressed and disenfranchised, the hungry, the homeless, the imprisoned, the ones who cannot read or write, also contain the world's most unevangelized and unreached people.

Illiteracy is powerfully linked to low social status, poverty, and poor health that are magnified for women, even women in the Church. Further, women who cannot read are blocked from reading the word of God. This barrier cripples them in their spiritual growth and in the spiritual training of their children.

The Church has the responsibility to uncover important insights about their community. Pictures of reality help the Church to make plans that are better suited to God's call upon it at this time and place. With this information, the Church can pursue renewed vitality and meaningful discipleship. The Church is ideally positioned to lead community efforts for awareness and action about adult illiteracy. Priority should be given to church-based programs for people groups with fifty percent or higher rates of illiteracy. The task is more likely to be achievable by working with one group at a time. The local church in any location can provide a service for the community, along with a powerful witness of the love, grace, and mercy of Christ.

Summary

The definition of literacy hinges on the functionality of what literacy does to a person and what a person does with literacy skills. Literacy makes it possible for individuals to sharpen their thinking skills. They are exposed to a world of information and abilities that help meet needs, achieve goals, and develop knowledge and potential. Such literacy skills can be used for personal and community development.

Adult illiteracy rates point out the great need to correct a serious global situation of male and female illiteracy. The information about Bangladesh shows that the illiteracy situation, though being corrected, would benefit from more positive efforts. A number of hindrances need to be overcome, such as women's access to education, negative attitudes and beliefs about literacy, lack of motivation, lack of availability of reading materials, and poor primary education.

Another challenge, not dealt with in this book, is a decline in reading habits. People who can read are not reading much, and this can be traced to the availability of television and other electronic distractions such as the internet. The lack of reading negatively affects the ability of a person to think and apply universal principles to local situations without prior experience.

Illiteracy has serious implications for communication in society and in the Church. It contributes to increasing crime rates, lower employment opportunities, lower income levels, and children not being sent to school. The Church's greatest challenge remains in evangelizing and discipling those who cannot read and write. Special attention should be given to women, who will teach their children about spiritual matters. Therefore, the Church should provide a base for literacy training in its immediate community.

CHAPTER 3

Adult Literacy Theory and Practice

In the 1960s, literacy was seen as the road to enlightenment. A more realistic attitude prevails after failed literacy campaigns and some successful ones. Even with a decrease in adult illiteracy rates seventeen percent of the world's adult population remains non-literate. The majority live in Africa and Asia (https://ourworldindata.org/literacy (accessed February 15, 2020)).

On the Church scene, since the Reformation, attempts to teach literacy in Western Europe have been successful. The initial motivation was to teach people to read the Bible (Arnove and Graff 1987:1-3). Likewise, in the early sixteenth century, European and North American missionaries in developing countries in Africa and Asia translated local languages into written form and also taught literacy as part of their strategy. The motivation was primarily the same—so that people could read the Bible for themselves (Coombs 1985:270).

Literacy campaigns and literacy programs differ: it is important not to confuse the two. Bhola, who was a prominent voice for UNESCO in adult education, notes that an education campaign is carried out on a large scale with a set of objectives that must be achieved within a certain time period. A literacy program similarly has a system with objectives to be achieved, but it may not have the same large size or urgency (1984:176).

The most famous mass literacy campaign happened in Cuba in 1961, linked to the country's political and social revolution. In nine months, over 700,000 adults were taught how to read, reducing the country's illiteracy rate by fifteen percent. That December, Fidel Castro was able to boast that Cuba was a country free of illiteracy. Amazingly, the official illiteracy rate continued to be a low one percent in Cuba (https://reason.com/ 2016/ 04/ 19/ cubas-literacy-rate-life-expectancy-noth/(accessed February 15, 2020)). Politically-driven literacy campaigns in Nicaragua and China have also been relatively effective in reducing illiteracy. Many other campaigns have reduced illiteracy rates. One of the major factors for success is funding.

Some literary campaigns fail because governments were unable to make an ongoing financial commitment after they started (Ahmed 1990:2). Another key reason for failure was that methods and content of literacy materials were not given due attention. For example, although the target group was adults, methods and content were for children. Other major factors include a lack of ongoing motivation after the initial excitement of participants; interest waned before the end of the literacy course (National Formal Education Information Center 1980). The primary reason given for such failures was that these campaigns were not placed in the larger context of a country's political and social situation (Ahmed 1990:2).

Paulo Freire

One literacy thinker who observed the connection between education and politics was Paulo Freire. In the early 1970s, Brazilian educator Paulo Freire published an English translation of his best-known work, *Pedagogy of the Oppressed*. In it, he critiqued the neutrality of formal education. He argued that "any curriculum that ignores racism, sexism, the exploitation of workers, and other forms of oppression supports the status quo. It inhibits the expansion of consciousness and blocks creative and liberating social action for change" (1990:23).

Freire's pedagogy found acceptance among many community-based adult learning proponents in South America. His critique of traditional schooling indicated that schools were part of the problem, "contributing to the marginalization of minorities and the poor" (1990:45). In Freire's view, education for liberation would challenge and enable learners to think about their current situation in the light of past history. It would cause an awakening in learners with an expectation of change and would seek expression in social reform and action, a beginning of a revolution (Mackie 1980:8). Taken to an extreme, there could be an uprising of common people against oppressive governments.

The Freirean Philosophy

The Freirean view of education was communal. There was strength in numbers and social change was accomplished in unity. When power was shared, it was not power for a few to improve themselves at the expense of others. Instead, the power of the many found strength and purpose in a common vision. Individuals could achieve liberation at the expense of others through an act of oppression. It was also true that personal freedom and the development of individuals could occur in communion with others. In the experience of many, groups—women who banded together, civil rights activists, and others committed to joint power—protected the individual far more than an authoritarian mode of organization (Adams 1975:78).

With shared power in learning, control was exercised over the curriculum, its contents and methods, and the coordination of all learning activities. This type of education provided a forum open to the discretion of the learners, the teachers, and the community. Empowerment became the means, as well as the outcome of this pedagogy, which has been called "liberation education" (Heaney 1989:3).

This liberation education is learning for empowerment. The content is both critical consciousness and the development of appropriate skills of literacy and in thinking. In this learning process, teachers and students are in dialogue, emphasizing that teachers and learners can be in conversation on equal footing (Miller 1985:21).

Critical Consciousness

Freire suggested three stages by which "critical consciousness" or "conscientization" is attained. The first stage was "semi-intransitive consciousness." "Intransitive" referred to a "passiveness or uncriticalness" of a person's consciousness. Therefore, semi-intransitive consciousness was the state of being when "perception is limited, whose interests center almost totally relate to matters of survival" (Freire 1990:32). Freire observed that as persons reach their potential to perceive and respond to suggestions and questions arising in their context, their capacity to enter into dialogue increased not only with others, but also with their own world—their consciousness became "transitive" (1990:33).

The second stage of consciousness was "naïve transitivity." At this stage, a person tended to over-simplify problems, had a nostalgia for the past, and did not want to face reality. Freire felt that naïve transitivity was never totally passed: it was a utopia people live in, which signified their sense of hope and optimism for a better tomorrow. For those who entered the learning process, naïve transitivity remained with them for life (1990:34).

The third and final stage in Freire's process was "critical transitivity." A person was able to interpret the seriousness of life challenges. For example, he or she tested his or her own conclusions, was willing to change if wrong, tried to get at the truth of the matter, avoided preconceptions, analyzed, was proactive, was open to new ideas without rejecting the old, and continuously dialogued with life (1990:35).

Here is an example of the three stages: eight Hispanic adults—three women and five men—gathered in a literacy class. One classmate arrives late, disturbed, and explains that her husband had threatened her. He argued that he does not want her going out to night classes and leaving her three children neglected. She left her home, with the argument with her husband unresolved, to resume her studies. Her teacher did not give any advice or encouragement to the woman, but instead asked the group for their opinion. Members of the class discussed their classmate's situation. They listed the following issues: a husband's "rights" over his wife, the acceptance of domestic violence against women as "normal," a presumption that women were "asking for trouble" if they go outside at night, and, that as a mother, their classmate had a major responsibility for her children (Heaney 1989:1).

The discussion in the class was energetic, with strong opinions for and against whether this issue reflected their culture and it was best to leave things the way they were. There was a growing solidarity among the women to argue for change. As the group continued discussing these issues, the teacher wrote some of the words they were using on the blackboard: "woman," "violence," "mother," and "wife"—word meanings the class has clarified themselves. Finally, the woman herself has shifted the focus of the group to the present reality and to a strategy for social transformation (Heaney 1989:1).

Institutionalization

Although Freire's theory gave hope to many community-based education proponents, his pedagogy—the practical, how-to-do-it methods—gave them the tools for the reconstruction of urban adult education. He advocated for dialogue and critical thinking, as opposed to an education that proposed that information was the "riches of knowledge . . . deposited in the empty vault of a learner's mind" without question. He used several pedagogical techniques in mass literacy campaigns that he organized in Brazil and Chile—campaigns that caused revolutionary social change. These techniques, incorporated by many literacy and basic education programs, included reflection on the political content of a learner's day-to-day experience, the organization of culture circles that promote dialogue and peer interaction, and the use of "people's knowledge" as the basis for curriculum (1990:48-50).

Even so, critique has been leveled at Freire's work, including his writing style, which seems confusing to many, and his concept of conscientization—that the poor need their consciousness to be raised—which seemed arrogant to his critics. One critic is Blanca Facundo: "The idea is not to judge Paulo Freire. We owe him justice and respect. For me, this means being as critical of his ideas and practices as he taught us to be critical of ours" (1984:n.p.).

Literacy work undertaken in or by community-based organizations has proven to be effective. The least effective programs are managed by formal schooling systems (Hunter and Harmon 1979:18). Literacy skills can be acquired more easily when linked with other development activities such as savings or income generation and if the outcome included changes in the conditions of an oppressed society (Shor 1987:76).

Freirean community-based adult education continues to provide a possible model for literacy programs. Liberation education links the problem of illiteracy with broader social and political ills, though it does not propose merely educational solutions to these problems. Adams agreed that there was hope for social action and change as a consequence of critical understanding by learners (Price-Karr 1975:103).

Frank Laubach

Frank Laubach's literacy method of "Each One Teach One" was built upon a discipleship model. This method was actually born when Laubach ran out of funding to pay literacy teachers in the Philippines. After Laubach told them that he could not pay them, a chieftain's response was to tell the teachers that he would kill them if they did not teach everyone how to read. This motivation brought fast results and each one taught someone else. Laubach felt that "Each One Teach One" was a better slogan than "each one, kill one" but he credited the chieftain for an original idea (1960:14).

Laubach (1884-1970) was one of the first to begin mass literacy campaigns in developing countries. As an American missionary working among the Filipino Maranao people, he was deeply concerned about the overwhelming poverty and injustice they suffered. He became convinced that the ability to read and write was essential for them to begin to solve their problems. Laubach planned his campaigns with church and government input. The main difference between his effort and those of other missionaries before him was that he saw literacy acquisition apart from the sole purpose of reading the Bible (Jennings 1990:29). Many knew him as the "Apostle to the Illiterates." Lowell Thomas called him "the foremost teacher of our times" (Laubach Literacy 1999:n.p.). The tribes of the Belgian Congo called him "Okombekombe," which means "mender of old baskets," because he taught adults to read and write (Laubach Literacy 1999:n.p.).

Using a basic instructional approach, Laubach found that even the most impoverished people could gain control of the written and spoken word. He discovered the potential of volunteers, newly literate Maranaos who taught adult learners through a one-to-one instructional program that became known as "Each One Teach One." Laubach also demonstrated that literacy was an effective means for positive community mobilization and change (1950:23).

Laubach Literacy

Over the course of about forty years, Laubach visited over one hundred countries to bring literacy to the "silent billion." His teams of visiting and local literacy workers worked tirelessly, field-testing teaching materials and techniques in the search for effective methods of teaching non-literate adults. Laubach was also a prolific writer and an accomplished speaker. He wrote forty books on prayer, literacy, justice, and world peace and spoke in meetings, inspiring congregations and community groups across the United States with his vision of a better world (SIL International—Lingualinks Library 4.0 2000).

In 1955, Laubach founded Laubach Literacy, a non-profit educational organization. His purpose was to enable non-literate adults and older youths to gain the listening, speaking, reading, writing, and math skills to solve problems they encountered in daily life. This would enable them to take full advantage of opportunities in their environment and to participate fully in the transformation of their society.

When asked what people could do to help, Laubach would say, "hunt out the deepest need you can find" (1950:88). Laubach spent his life and boundless energy on behalf of the world's neediest people, motivating hundreds of thousands to join him in service to humanity. His work left an indelible mark on the twentieth century and offers messages of hope to future generations as they carry on the work of building a literate, just, and peaceful world. He also said,

> A literate person is not only an illiterate person who has learned to read and write—he [or she] is another person. He [or she] is different. To promote literacy is to change man's [or woman's] conscience by changing his [or her] relation to his [or her] environment. It is an undertaking on the same

plane as the recognition and incarnation of fundamental human rights (1950:115).

The Laubach Method

The Laubach Method uses the following principles:

1. Letter-sound relationships are established. Letters of an alphabet system and sounds they stand for are taught in a systematic manner. It uses existing phonetic regularities, emphasizes regular spellings, and provides help to know irregular spellings.
2. Learning is done through association. Letters and sounds are presented through key words with picture associations. The pictures represent the shape and sound of a letter. For example, a picture of a snake could help in learning the letter "S" and its sound.
3. Teaching is done from known information to unknown or new information. It begins with the spoken word which is known by the learner, and then slowly progresses to the written word, which is not known.
4. Familiar vocabulary is used. These are words used in the spoken vocabulary of the adult learner. The vocabulary is controlled, with a limited number of new words in each lesson so that the learner is not overwhelmed by the new words.
5. Repetition strengthens the grasp of the student of the new words. So, in each lesson, each word and sentence is repeated several times soon after it is taught.
6. The content of the lessons is relevant to life.
7. In each lesson there is something new to be learned. However, the new word or sentence is introduced in a familiar lesson pattern.
8. Independent learning is stressed. The way the lesson is set up—visual aids, phonetic skills, consistent lesson patterns, and uniformity of format—lends itself to the learner helping himself or herself in the pursuit of literacy skills.
9. The lessons are easy to teach. They are planned for maximum self-help and minimum teacher-help. Detailed teaching manuals

make it possible for inexperienced teachers to use the materials successfully (1950:125).

Laubach's teaching methodology affirmed the learner. More than the teaching methodology, Laubach concentrated on people. He loved the underprivileged and hungry. He emphasized developing suitable reading materials but realized that this was weak in his earlier literacy campaigns. His hope was to train nationals in writing simple stories.[1]

Sarah Gudschinsky

Sarah Gudschinsky also contributed to the theory on literacy. Unlike Freire, she stayed away from political involvement. Her method was built upon Laubach's but took linguistic principles even further.

Gudschinsky (1919-1974) was a researcher, innovator, and scholar in the specialized field of introducing literacy to preliterate societies. As a member of Summer Institute of Linguistics, she worked with the Mazatec people of Mexico. She was a linguistic and literacy consultant as well as serving SIL as International Literacy Coordinator. She developed a reading approach that has since been named for her.

The Gudschinsky Method

The Gudschinsky method has also been called "the focusing method," "the five-step method," "a fully linguistic method," and "a whole language method" (Lee 1982:476). These different names describe components of her method. It can be called "the focusing method" because of its use of "focusing drills." These drills could focus on a particular syllable but that syllable would not appear out of the context of a word or sentence. It can be called "the five-step method" because of the five steps in the basic drills for teaching letters: analysis, synthesis, identification, contrast, and word building. Gudschinsky called it "the fully linguistic method" because "it attempts to take every

---

[1] This is not to say that Laubach's method is guaranteed to work in all circumstances. In Liberia, a national literacy program under Laubach launched in 1950 but soon dissipated (Johnson 2001).

aspect of the linguistic structure of language into account in teaching reading and writing" (Lee 1982:476). Lee labeled it "the whole language method" for two reasons:

The first was that many people had been disillusioned by earlier "linguistic" methods which focused primarily on only one aspect of the linguistic structure of language, namely, sound-symbol relationships. This is not to say that these methods did not have merit, but many people expected them to solve all of the reading problems and when they did not, people tended to reject what they called "the linguistic method." The second reason was that the term language is easier to understand than the term linguistic. The word linguistic may mean one thing to the professional linguist and quite another thing to the non-linguist. Learning to read is commonly referred to as a language art and appropriately so since reading is one use of language. It seemed that a reading method which utilized every aspect of language could appropriately be called a whole language method (1982:477).

There were two major divisions in the Gudschinsky method—reading and writing. Each division had three subdivisions. The reading division included letter drills, functor drills, and the reading of connected material. In the writing division, the three subdivisions were letter formation, spelling, and creative writing (Lee 1982:478).

The goals of reading acquisition included reading independently, with comprehension, and with fluency. To attain these goals, certain skills needed to be learned. These skills were kept in mind in the design of drills on letters, functors, and the reading of connected material. Letter drills focused primarily on teaching mediated word identification while the functor drills focused on immediate word identification. The connected material gave opportunity for both plus immediate meaning identification through the use of context.

Assessing Literacy to Pre-Literates

There are two main arguments against introducing literacy to the so-called "pre-literate societies." The first is that literacy causes change to culture and language. Second, literacy can be used as a control to maintain uneven social relationships by keeping the power in the hands of the "educated" and away from the non-literate in society (Tauchi 2000:n.p.).

The Need for a New Approach

By the mid-nineties, Zeilyn noted the need for a new approach that integrated the strengths of the existing methods with new dimensions. In his book, *Appropriate Media for Training and Development*, Zeitlyn says,

> The development of an appropriate communication and training technology is essential if people in third world countries are going to take up development of projects and overcome the problems of passing on skills and ideas to those rural people who really need them. Overcoming the barriers of isolation and lack of education found in the countryside requires appropriate techniques and media as well as resources. Without them the development expertise leaves with the experts and the development cannot be sustained (1995:1).

Taking the Best from These Methods

Freire's radical literacy approach had some useful salient features. It was highly motivational through his concept of raising a person's critical consciousness of his or her environment. Another strong point was an emphasis on the community, whereby literacy becomes shared knowledge that benefitted a group rather than an individual at any one time.

Laubach emphasized the sharing of literacy skill from one person to another. Laubach's way of reading was simple to use and easily adapted to new situations. As a systematic method, it built on each learner's capability, making learning relevant. His methods also stressed another important aspect—the independence of learning.

Gudschinsky, on the other hand, developed a systematic and thorough method that deals with any language holistically. She considered linguistic aspects of structure when teaching reading and writing. Her goals were that a learner could read independently, with comprehension, and with fluency.

Using Media

Digital media was not included in the methodologies Freire, Laubach, and Gudschinsky developed. However, media is an excellent motivational tool. Learners can repeat lessons consistently. Media can help explain the structure of language or give the necessary context. An article in *Literacy Innovations* stated, "Technology will play a major role in transforming of lifelong learning into a reality" (1996-1997:1). Similarly, Harvey T. Hoekstra commented about the potential of using audio products in literacy programs:

There is tremendous potential of an audio product for that whole range of non-formal education programs in the areas of public health, agriculture and development, and literacy. With solar power, exciting programs involving long hours of playing time are now possible. Literacy programs geared to audio products enable people to learn to read with a minimum of specialized teaching other than those few initial lessons to ensure that the correlation between primer and learner and listening is understood (1982:42).

An article on literacy and the use of media noted a number of important points about technology (*Literacy Innovations* 1996-1997:2):

1. Even though cost is an issue, the most difficult and expensive issue is human and not technical. Audio products can take the role of the teacher, saving money that go towards salaries and providing numerous possibilities for expansion.
2. The rapid expansion of media such as audio products, radio, video, television, and the internet has a profound effect on the creation and dissemination of knowledge. Focus has shifted from teaching to learning and from classrooms to communities, the market-place, and the home. Rethinking the transmission of content, learning how to learn, and skills in the management of information is vital.

3. Developing countries may not have the same type of technology as industrialized countries, but they need to have appropriate technologies as defined by their unique economic and cultural situations. Those planning literacy and educational programs should include in their budgets expenditures for necessary equipment to fulfill their strategic plans, keeping in mind the selection of a media that fits the needs of the people.
4. Determining the role of technology in a literacy program is a challenging, complex process. It is wise to compare and share experiences from countries with similar conditions for managing the challenges and realizing the potential of technology for literacy training and lifelong learning.

Summary

Three main contributors to literacy theory include Freire, who used a liberation approach to education within community-based literacy programs. He said those in his literacy system would be motivated as their critical consciousness awakened to the oppression they were in, causing a reaction that would lead to social reform and action. His methodology highly motivated most of the learners in literacy learning to seek liberation from their oppressive conditions.

Laubach used a relational approach, so that each person taught would teach yet another person. In this way, literacy was multiplied. His teaching method for reading was built upon letter-sound relationships and association with pictures that represented the shape and sound of a particular letter. His methodology guided a learner from the place he or she is, used familiar vocabulary, built on lessons that were meaningful, and could be learned independently.

Gudschinsky used a linguistic approach to teach literacy skills of reading and writing. Her methodology was built on drills for teaching letters, which helped the learner analyze, synthesize, identify, contrast, and do word building exercises. The Gudschinsky method took into consideration how a person learns to read and write. Her educational goals were independence, comprehension, and fluency.

The long-term results of these older literacy programs were not as encouraging. A new approach must integrate the strengths of the effective parts of other approaches. Motivation, community mobilization, logistics of teaching the whole language, and the usage of appropriate media should be addressed. Budgets should cover the provision of equipment and training of people to use the technology. Proper planning should shape how the lesson content is to be transmitted and information to be managed. It is also imperative to take into account the experiences of other countries struggling with the challenges of illiteracy.

CHAPTER 4

Historical Aspects and Influences

Literacy is not accomplished in a vacuum: people live in multifaceted contexts. In this study, six contextual aspects in Bangladesh will be considered: history, religion, sociopolitical, cultural arts, education, and the influence of media.

The nation of Bangladesh emerged from an old country with a rich history. It was recognized as an independent country in 1971. Its history stems from ancient times, followed by conquest by Mongols, Persians, Turks, and Afghans. Muslims ruled the region from the thirteenth until the eighteenth century, after which the British occupied the Indian subcontinent for two hundred years. In 1947, the British partitioned the subcontinent according to religion into two sovereign states: India and Pakistan. After twenty-one years and a short but violent war, Bangladesh was born on March 26, 1971 (DW Corp Ltd. 1999:n.p.).

Islam is the dominant religion in Bangladesh, with pockets of Hindus, Buddhists, Christians, and animists. The official percentage of Christians is so low that they are grouped into "other religions." Each religion does not give equal value to literacy. Islam and Christianity, for example, use special holy books. By default, this raises the value of reading. Other religions may not regard literacy in the same way.

Several major political groups function in Bangladesh. The present ruling political party is the Awami League (AL). However, there are many opposition party members in the Parliament (https://freedom house.org/report/freedom-world/2019/bangladesh(accessed February 15, 2020)).

Bangladesh's rich culture is expressed in music, dance, literature, and art. Culturally, Bengali is the heart language spoken by the largest number of people—100 million in west Bengal and 160 million in

Bangladesh. It is the sixth most spoken language by native speakers in the world. Bengali belongs to the Aryan branch of the Indo-European family of languages and has existed as an independent language for more than ten centuries (Bengali at Ethnologue, 22nd edition, 2019 (accessed February 15, 2020)). Education is a challenge in Bangladesh, so it is important to understand the condition of general education as well as that of adult education.

Mass media is still a luxury of the rich. It is hardly likely that a rural farmer has touched a computer, although cell phones are easily available to Bangladeshis.

Historical Aspects of Bangladesh

The British divided the subcontinent of India into India and (West and East) Pakistan on August 15, 1947. Islam linked the two parts of Pakistan but language, ethnic, and cultural differences were not considered. These later became issues for separation (Heitzman and Worden 1989:1). By 1971, civil war in Pakistan resulted in the separation of and renaming of East Pakistan. Thus, Bangladesh was born, with a homogenous people who shared a similar language, culture, and ethnicity.

India and Bhutan were among the first countries to recognize Bangladesh. The Pakistani war ravaged the country and left Bangladesh impoverished, low on resources, and economically crippled. In 1972, Henry Kissinger gave it the unfortunate label of "international basket case" (Education in Bangladesh 2000:n.p.).

However, Bangladeshis celebrated their independence and offered their loyalty to the first national leader, Sheikh Mujibur Rahman (Mujib), or the Bangabandhu (the "Beloved of Bangladesh"), who gave his life for his newborn country. The future of Bangladesh, envisioned by the Bangabandhu and enshrined in the 1972 Constitution as nationalism, socialism, secularism, and democracy, was uncertain and unpredictable. In 1975, Mujib was assassinated along with most of his family members. Two daughters were spared; one later became the prime minister. History repeated itself with the assassination of President Ziaur Rahman and the subsequent ousting of President H. M. Ershad.

The Early History and Mughal Period (1000 BC-AD 1757)

Four historical periods have formed Bangladesh (Jacob 1997:35). According to Hasna Jasimuddin Moudud, there is little recorded of the history of ancient Bengal, thus making her history the "most complex in the world" (n.d.:n.p). The recorded history of Bengal begins in the fourth century BC.

In the third century BC, Bangladesh formed part of the extensive Mauryan kingdom. Through the end of twelfth century, the great Mauryans, Guptas, the Palas and Sena kings, successfully ruled the northern and western parts. Muslims overthrew the last monarch's rule in 1204 AD (Franda 1982:4).

In 500 AD, the Pal Dynasty brought a golden beginning to the political history of Bengal. Puthis of that era used alphabets and drawings. The oldest known poets, Kahupad and Bhushuk, belonged to the eighth and ninth centuries AD. Bhushuk first used the word "Bengali" in his poetry. Between 1415-1417 AD, during the reign of King Ganesh, one can find the evidence of Bengali alphabets on coins (Baxter 1984:20).

Turks ruled Bengal for several decades before the conquest of Dhaka by forces of the Mughal emperor, Akbar the Great (1556-1605) in 1576. Bengal remained a Mughal province until the beginning of the decline of the Mughal Empire in the eighteenth century. Bengal was probably the wealthiest part of the subcontinent until the sixteenth century. The Mughals had a profound and lasting effect on Bengal economy and religion. Akbar the Great introduced the present-day Bengali calendar. His son Jahangir (1605-1627) put into place rights to collect taxes on land by civil and military officials from outside Bengal. This led to the development of the *zamindar* class, who were the tax collectors and landlords. The British used this system to rule Bengal, also known as the "breadbasket of India" (Majumdar 1943:74).

The European Period (1757-1857)

The British East India Company, a private company, was already formed in 1600 during the reign of Akbar. It operated under a charter granted by Queen Elizabeth I. This company established a factory on the Hooghly River in Bengal in 1650 and founded the city of Calcutta in 1690. The initial aim of the British East India Company was to seek trade under concessions obtained from local Mughal governors. Yet the steady collapse of the Mughal Empire (1526-1858) enticed the company to become more directly involved in the politics and military activities of the subcontinent. They capitalized on the political fragmentation of South Asia. They left the Indian social institutions untouched, but a number of Anglican and Baptist evangelicals in Britain felt that social institutions should be reformed (Thapar 1966:105).

Pressured by the homeland, British administrators in India embarked on social and administrative reforms. Emphasis was placed on the introduction of Western philosophy, technology, and institutions rather than on the reconstruction of native institutions. The early attempts by the British East India Company to encourage the use of Sanskrit and Persian were abandoned in favor of Western science and literature. Elementary education was taught in the vernacular, but higher education in English. The stated purpose of secular education was to produce a class of Indians instilled with British cultural values. Persian was replaced with English as the official language of the government. In the field of social reforms, the British suppressed what they considered to be inhumane practices, such as *suttee*—the burning of widows on the funeral pyres of their husbands—female infanticide, and human sacrifice (Mascarenhas 1986:46).

On May 10, 1857, Indian soldiers of the British Indian Army, drawn mostly from Muslim units from Bengal mutinied and started a year-long insurrection against the British. The mutiny was sparked by a rumor that cartridges given to the soldiers were greased with pig or cow fat, which were considered religiously unclean to both Muslims and Hindus (Spear 2018: n.p). The soldiers marched to Delhi and offered their services to the Mughal emperor, whose predecessors had been defeated one hundred years earlier at Plassey. Historians have called this uprising the Soldiers' Rebellion, the Great Mutiny, and the Revolt of 1857. Many people of the subcontinent call it India's "first war of independence."

The Nationalist Movement and the Rise of Muslim Consciousness (1857-1947)

Recognition of the Muslim community from its low status after the 1857 mutiny was a gradual process throughout the ensuing century. In education, commerce, and government service, Muslims lagged behind Hindus, who more quickly adapted to rapidly changing socioeconomic conditions. Sir Syed Ahmad Khan (1817-1898), a Muslim noble and writer, influenced the reconciliation of the traditional views of Indian Muslims, the new ideas, and the education system introduced by the British. Syed was responsible for the founding in 1875 of the Muhammadan-Anglo Oriental College. In this college, Islamic culture and religious instruction were combined with a British university system. Syed was one of the first Muslims to recognize the problems facing his community under a government ruled by the Hindu majority. He warned that safeguards were necessary to avoid the possibility of open violence between the religious communities of India (Baxter 1984:79).

In 1905, the British governor-general, Lord George Curzon, divided Bengal into eastern and western sectors. Curzon established a new province called Eastern Bengal and Assam, with its capital at Dhaka. The new province of West had its capital at Calcutta, which also was the capital of British India.

During the next few years, the long neglected and predominantly Muslim eastern region of Bengal made strides in education and communications (Basham 1954:63). Muslims generally favored the partition of Bengal but could not compete with the more politically articulate and economically powerful Hindus. In 1912, the British voided the partition of Bengal, a decision that heightened the growing estrangement between the Muslims and Hindus in many parts of the country. Muslims perceived the reunion of divided Bengal as a British accommodation to Hindu pressures (O'Donnell 1984:39). Finally, on August 14, 1947, the British gave independence to Pakistan. On March 21, 1948, Mohammed Ali Jinnah, the first governor-general, declared at a public meeting in Dhaka, "Urdu shall be the state language of Pakistan" (Burki 1986:80).

The Language Movement (1952), the War of Liberation (1970-1971), and the New Nation of Bangladesh

On February 21, 1952, university students came out to the streets in protest, demanding Bengali as the state language. Police retaliated by killing Salam, Barkat, Rafiq, and Jabber, who were considered martyrs for the cause. This was called the "Language Movement." On September 5-6, 1966, the politicians of West Pakistan organized a conference of different political parties in Pakistan. On that occasion, Sheik Mujibur Rahman, general secretary of the East Pakistan Awami League, presented the famous six-points demand outlining full autonomy for East Pakistan. Unfortunately, the West Pakistani leaders openly discarded the six-points demand, declared Sheikh Mujibur Rahman as a separatist, and arrested him (Maniruzzaman 1980:28). The United Nations have set February 21st an International Mother Language Day.

This escalated into a liberation force of common people who formed a disciplined and determined army. On April 17, 1971, in Mujibnagar, in the district of Kushtia, the Provisional Government was formed and took the oath of office. The international media, overwhelmed with the struggle of the Bengali people, extended their sympathy and full support. The War of Liberation was won because the people wholeheartedly wanted freedom. The Mukti Bahini, liberation fighters consisting of the common people, found shelter, food, and information from people in the rural areas wherever they went. However, Bengalis paid victory's price in blood (Mascarenhas 1986:114).

CHAPTER 5

Religious Aspects and Influences

Just to recap, about ninety percent of Bangladeshis are Muslims, making Bangladesh one of the largest Muslim countries, with a population of approximately 168 million. Hinduism is professed by ten percent of the population. There are smaller numbers of Buddhist, indigenous tribal religions as well as Christians. Together these two groups are estimated to share the remaining one percent in Bangladesh.

Islam in Bangladesh

Islam reached Bangladesh in the thirteenth century and was established as the state religion in 1988. Conversion was generally collective rather than individual. Islamic egalitarianism, especially the ideals of equality and social justice, attracted numerous Buddhists and lower caste Hindus. Muslim mystics wandered about in villages and were responsible for many conversions (Aid to the Church in Need 1998:n.p.).

Most Muslims in Bangladesh are Sunnis, a mystical type of Islam, but there is also a small Shia community. The tradition of Islamic mysticism known as Sufism appeared early in Islam and became a popular movement emphasizing love of God rather than fear of God. Sufism stresses a direct, unstructured, and personal devotion to God in place of the ritualistic, outward observance of the faith. An important belief in the Sufi tradition is that the average believer may use spiritual guides in his or her pursuit of the truth. These guides—friends of God or saints—are commonly called *fakirs* or *pirs*. In Bangladesh, the term "*pir*" is more commonly used and combines the meanings of teacher and saint. They often use music called *ghazals* and *qawwali* dance. The largest Sunni gathering, and the second largest Muslim gathering after the *Hajji* to Mecca, called *Biswa Ijtema* is held annually in January for three days, in Tongi, Dhaka Distict (Kamaluddin 1988:41, https://www.telegraph.co.uk/news/worldnews/asia/bangladesh/12088120/What-is-the-festival-of-Bishwa-Ijtema-and-where-is-itheld.html (accessed February 15, 2020)).

The Quran is the scripture of Islam, a religion established by Muhammad. Other sayings and teachings of Muhammad and his key followers, as well as the examples of his personal behavior, became the *hadith*. Together they form the Muslim's comprehensive guide to spiritual, ethical, and social living. The *shahadah*, or testimony, succinctly states the central belief of Islam, "There is no god but God (Allah), and Muhammad is his Prophet." Islam means "submission to God," and he or she who submits is a Muslim (Akter 1992:58).

"Five pillars" of the faith are the duties of the Muslim: recitation of the testimony (*shahadah*; in Bangla, *kalima*), daily prayer (*salat*; in Bangla, *namaj*), almsgiving (*zakat*; in Bangla, *jakat*), fasting (*sawm*; in Bangla, *roja*), and pilgrimage (*hajj*). The testimony is repeatedly recited by Bengali Muslims. The devout believer prays after purification, at dawn, midday, mid-afternoon, sunset, and nightfall facing Mecca (Abecassis 1990:43). Public prayer is a conspicuous and widely practiced aspect of Islam in Bangladesh (Kabeer 1991:38-42). Almsgiving (donations to the poor) is voluntary but expected (Ahamed and Nazneen 1990:14). The ninth month of the Muslim calendar, Ramadan, is a period of obligatory fasting. Finally, Islam dictates that at least once in his or her lifetime a Muslim should, if possible, make the *hajj* to Mecca to participate in special rites held there during the twelfth month of the Muslim calendar (Alam 1993:19).

Hinduism in Bangladesh

Unlike Islam, Hinduism lacks a single authoritative scripture. Hindus are not required to read the *Bhagavad-gita* and it has no historically known author. The term Hinduism applies to a large number of diverse beliefs and practices. In a sense, Hinduism is a synthesis of the religious expression of the people of South Asia and an anonymous expression of their worldview and cosmology, rather than the articulation of a particular creed. However, the Hindu religion in Bangladesh can best be understood in a regional context in terms of the caste system, beliefs, rituals, and festivals of the Hindus (Baxter and Rahman 1989:356).

A distinction has sometimes been made between the religion of the "great tradition" and the popular religion of the "little tradition." The great tradition, sometimes called Brahmanism, developed under the leadership of Hinduism's highest caste group, the Brahmans. As Hinduism's traditional priests, teachers, and astrologers, Brahmans enjoy numerous social privileges. The great tradition preserves refined and abstract philosophical concepts that exhibit little regional variation. At this level, there is emphasis on unity in diversity and a pervasive attitude of relativism (Robinson 1989:57).

The great tradition recognizes a trinity of gods, who are actually forms of absolute Brahman: Brahma the creator, Vishnu the preserver, and Shiva the destroyer. The worship of Shiva generally finds adherents among the higher castes in Bangladesh. Worship of Vishnu more explicitly cuts across caste lines by teaching the fundamental oneness of humankind in spirit. Vishnu worship in Bengal expresses the union of the male and female principles in a tradition of love and devotion. This form of Hindu belief and the Sufi tradition of Islam have influenced and interacted with each other in Bengal. Both were popular mystical movements emphasizing the personal relationship of religious leader and disciple, in contrast to the dry stereotypes of the Brahmans or the *ulama*, a Muslim religious leader. As in Bengali Islamic practice, worship of Vishnu frequently occurs in a small devotional society or *samaj* (Lipner 1994:80).

On the level of tradition, Hinduism involves worship of spirits and godlings of rivers, mountains, vegetation, animals, stones, or disease. Ritual bathing, vows, and pilgrimages to sacred rivers, mountains, shrines, and cities are important practices. An ordinary Hindu will worship at the shrines of Muslim *pirs* without being concerned with the religion to which that place is supposed to be affiliated. Hindus revere many holy men and ascetics who are conspicuous for their bodily mortifications. Some people believe they attain spiritual benefit merely by looking at a great holy man (Walker 1995:137).

In the late 1980s, Hindus were almost evenly distributed in all regions, with concentrations in Khulna, Jessore, Dinajpur, Faridpur, and Barisal. The contributions of Hindus in arts and letters far exceeded their numerical strength. In politics, they traditionally supported the liberal and secular ideology of the Awami League. Hindu institutions and places of worship received assistance through the Bangladesh Hindu Kalyan Trust (Bangladesh Hindu Welfare Trust), which was sponsored by the Ministry of Religious Affairs. Government-sponsored television and radio also broadcast readings and interpretations of Hindu scriptures and prayers (Johnson 1996:68).

Buddhism in Bangladesh

Buddhism in various forms appears to have been prevalent at the time of the Turkish conquest of Bangladesh in 1202. The invading armies apparently found numerous monasteries, which they destroyed in the belief that they were military fortresses. With the destruction of its centers of learning, Buddhism rapidly disintegrated. In subsequent centuries, through the 1980s, nearly all remaining Buddhists lived in the region around Chittagong, which had not been entirely conquered until the time of the British Raj. In the Chittagong Hills, Buddhist tribes formed the majority of the population. Their religion appeared to be a mixture of tribal cults and Buddhist teaching.

There are several monasteries in the Chittagong Hills area. There is a school in most Buddhist villages where boys live and learn to read Burmese and some Pali, an ancient Buddhist scriptural language. It is common for men who have finished their schooling to return at regular intervals for periods of residence in the school (Barua 2001:n.p.). The Ministry of Religious Affairs provides assistance for the maintenance of Buddhist places of worship and relics. Ancient monasteries have been discovered in Paharpur, Rajshahi, and Mainamati in Comilla, dating from the seventh to ninth centuries AD.

Christianity in Bangladesh

Christianity's first contact with the Indian subcontinent is attributed to the Apostle Thomas, who is said to have preached in southern India in 52 AD. Although Jesuit priests were active at the Mughal courts in the sixteenth and seventeenth centuries, the first Roman Catholic settlements in Bangladesh appear to have been established by the Portuguese. During the sixteenth century, the Portuguese settled in the vicinity of Chittagong, where they were active in piracy and slave trading. In the seventeenth century, some Portuguese moved to Dhaka. Even today, those of Portuguese-converted Catholic descent have Portuguese-sounding surnames (D'Costa n.d:n.p.).

The Ministry of Religious Affairs provided assistance and support to the Christian institutions in the country. In the late 1980s, the government was not imposing restrictions on the legitimate religious activities of the missions and the communities. Mission schools and hospitals were well attended and were used by members of all religions. The Christian community usually enjoyed better opportunities for education and a better standard of living. In the late 1980s, Christianity had about 600,000 adherents, mainly Roman Catholic, and their numbers were growing rapidly (D'Costa n.d:n.p.).

Protestant missionary efforts began only in the first half of the nineteenth century. Baptist missionary activities began in 1816, followed by the Anglican Oxford Mission. Other missions worked mainly among the tribal peoples of the "Low Hills" in the northern part of Mymensingh and Sylhet regions. Many Christian churches, schools, and hospitals were initially set up to serve the European community, but they subsequently became centers of conversion as they served Bengalis. Particularly, there were conversions among the lower caste Hindus (D'Costa n.d.:n.p.).

Problems and Needs in the Church in Bangladesh

There is a small but significant population of Christians in Bangladesh with point five percent of the population, or about 800,000 believers in a country of over 160 million people. Between 400,000 to 450,000 are Roman Catholic, and the remaining 250,000 to 400,000 are divided among 51 different denominations (Speicher 2002:n.p.). Low literacy levels and lack of education are national and community concerns (Council for World Mission 2002:n.p.). The following profile was written by Open Doors International (2002:n.p.) about the problems and needs in Bangladesh:

1. There are strong divisions between churches of Christians who converted from Hinduism and those who converted from Islam. Christians in Bangladesh are either converts from Hindu or tribal religions and have little inclination of reaching out to Muslim Bengalis. There are also divisions along tribal/ethnic lines. If there are any converts from Islam into Christianity, these converts are met with suspicion by Christians in the existing churches.
2. There is an aversion to reaching out to Muslims among existing churches as mentioned above. As such there are some Muslim converts who are working within Muslim communities to stimulate a movement of Muslims who have become believers in *Isa* or the Messiah.
3. Much of the pastoral leadership of the church is done on a part-time basis. Churches are not able to pay a wage to their pastors, thus, pastors have to work another job to support themselves and their families.
4. There is poverty in the existing churches, which make them dependent on foreign aid.
5. There is a lack of well-trained leadership. Poverty hinders Christians who are called to ministry from studying at a Bible school or seminary full-time.
6. For those who are trained and qualified pastors, there is a lack of advanced training materials and other Christian books in order to improve themselves.
7. There is division along denominational lines and, in some cases, a lack of cooperation between churches.

Speicher adds that the percentage of Christians has not changed much but new denominations are luring members from older churches. She also says that poverty among Christians has caused them to change denominations, as the new churches offer special benefits such as stipends for their children or jobs for themselves (Speicher 2002:n.p.). However, there is an attempt to build an understanding of ecumenism among the churches. In a March 2001 statement by the general secretary of the World Council of Churches, Konrad Raiser challenged churches "to overcome such distrust and rivalry and strengthen opportunities to work cooperatively" (Speicher 2002:n.p.).

The Bangladesh Bible Society

William Carey, a famous Protestant missionary, translated the Bible in 1833 and compiled *A Dictionary of the Bengali Language* (William Carey College n.d.:n.p.). The rich heritage of Bible work in Bangladesh dates back to the efforts of Carey:

> The history of the Bible Society of undivided Bengal started in the year 1801 through the untiring efforts of Dr. William Carey. The Old and New Testaments of the Bible were translated and revised with the initiative of various missionary institutions up to 1909. The Bible Society of Calcutta was formed in 1911. The East Pakistan Bible Society was formed in 1953 and was managed by the Pakistan Bible Society located in Lahore. In 1966, the East Pakistan Bible Society became directly affiliated with the UBS and started functioning independently. In the year 1971, after the liberation war, the East Pakistan Bible Society emerged as the Bangladesh Bible Society (Bangladesh Bible Society 2001a:n.p.).

The translation of the Bible by Carey is a highly-prized literary book. In its literary form, even some well-educated people are not able to understand all the words used in the Carey translation. Between 1979 and 1981, the Bangladesh Bible Society in cooperation with the Association of Baptist World Evangelism (ABWE) began translating the New Testament into commonly used Bengali that is easier to understand. Presently, the whole Bible is available in both Muslimani and standard Bengali (Bangladesh Bible Society 2001b: n.p.).

The BBS employs office workers to provide services from the main office in Dhaka and distribution workers to reach the far corners of the country. In 1979, to address the challenge of the non-literate population of the country, audio products were produced with portions from the Scriptures for people those who do not know how to read or write. Audio products with Scriptures-in-song and reflective readings were produced and made available in the tribal language of Santali, as well as special target groups, such as the blind. In particular, two series of audio products called *Shukhobor* (Good News) and *Muktir Path* (Path of Salvation) were recorded for audiences who are new readers (Chai 2000:11). The Bangladesh Bible Society now has phone apps with Audio Bibles (http://biblesociety.org.bd/category/apps/(accessed February 15, 2020)).

Bangladesh Lutheran Church

According to D'Costa, other Protestant missions that arrived after Carey included the Lutheran Santal Mission in 1956 (D'Costa n.d:n.p.). In the 1970s, just after the War of Liberation, the Danish Santal Mission (DSM) began relief and rehabilitation work in the northwestern part of Bangladesh. Four Lutheran mission organizations from four different countries (America, Denmark, Finland, and Norway) later formed the Bangladesh Lutheran Mission (BLM). In the beginning, the BLM was mainly associated with the Bangladesh Northern Evangelical Lutheran Church (BNELC), which is primarily a Santali church. However, missionaries also went to Hindu villages, resulting in converts from the Rajbanis and other Hindu low castes. Since Bengali Christians had different cultural and language traditions, they wanted their autonomy. So, in 1979, the Bangladesh Lutheran Church (BLC) was founded with seventy members and was supported by DSM. The mission established a boarding school and three mission compounds. DSM also registered as a non-governmental organization (NGO) under the name Bangladesh Lutheran Mission—Danish (BLM-D) to do development work. BLM-D's strategy, however, was to work where there were existing BLC congregations to benefit them through development work. The goal was that BLC would become an independent church as the members grew more self-sufficient (Schrøder 1993:1).

Currently, the BLC has 6,200 members (https://www.lutheran-world.org/ content/bangladesh-lutheran-church(accessed February 15,

2020)). It has been a member of the Lutheran World Federation (LWF) since 1981. In 1992, four pastors graduated from CCTB with bachelor degrees in theology (BTh). Other village pastors and church members have enrolled in various levels of theological education by extension (Evangelical Lutheran Church in America Division for Global Mission n.d.:n.p.). The BLC faces several unique challenges as explained by Flemming Schrøder (1993:3), a former missionary of BLM-D:

1. BLC congregations are geographically widespread making travel to each congregation difficult.
2. Each congregation is small, consisting of three to twelve families.
3. BLC members are among the poorest of the poor.
4. BLC members face opposition from Hindus in their village, such as denial of access to drinking water and even expulsion from their families.
5. Responsibility for Christian education of church members lies on the congregational leader or pastor. Many of the new converts were baptized after only a few weeks of catechism, so they have little understanding of their new life in Christ and how this affects their daily life. There are approximately thirty ordained pastors, half of whom have little or no formal education, and some of which are functionally non-literate.
6. It is estimated that eighty percent of BLC members are non-literate.
7. BLC is still dependent on the mission to fund church activities.

BLC needed literacy training and Bible education to disciple their church leaders and members, as well as a means of outreach to their surrounding communities. Many BLC village pastors were new readers who were not able to read the New Testament fluently and had done little reading in the Old Testament. Its denominational members were not able to read the Word of God. BLC members lived in villages, which were primarily Hindu. Literacy training would be an opportunity to expose the villagers to the gospel.

In the 1990s, the BBS partnered with BLC in a pilot literacy program that used Scripture. Through BLM-D, villages with BLC members and their Hindu neighbors, some of who had been through basic literacy training, formed the core of the literacy groups in this experiment (Chai 2000:2).

Animism in Bangladesh

Tribal groups constitute less than one percent of the total population and the majority live in rural areas of the Chittagong Hills and in the regions of Mymensingh, Sylhet, and Rajshahi. They differ from the rest of the country in their social organization, marriage customs, birth and death rites, food, and other social customs. Their languages originate from Tibet and Myanmar. In the mid-1980s, the percentage distribution of tribal population by religion was twenty four percent Hindu, forty-four percent Buddhist, thirteen percent Christian, and nineteen percent animist (Bangladesh Development Gateway 2001:n.p.).

Major tribes are the Chakmas, Maghs (or Marmas), Tipras, Murangs, Kukis, and Santals. The tribes tend to intermingle and are distinguished from one another more by differences in their dialect, dress, and customs, rather than by tribal cohesion. Only the Chakmas and Marmas display formal tribal organization. These are of mixed origin but reflect more Bengali influence than any of the other tribes. Unlike the other tribes, the Chakmas and Marmas generally live in the highland valleys. Most Chakmas are Buddhist but some practice Hinduism or animism.

The Santals live in the northwestern part of Bangladesh and obey a set of religious beliefs similar to Hinduism. The Khasais live in Sylhet in the Khasia Hills near the border with Assam; the Garo and Hajang live in the northeastern part of the country. The literacy rate among tribal groups is thirty-eight percent for males and forty-nine percent for females. The high rate among women is due to matrilineal nature of these societies.

Ferdaus Quarishi, a political journalist, wrote *Christianity in the North Eastern Hills of South Asia: Social Impact and Political Implications*, which traces the population explosion of the tribal groups in the northeastern tip of the South Asian subcontinent. He lists several tribal groups: Nagas, Mizos, Khasis, and Manipuris, as well Bangladesh's Tripuris, Ahoms, and Chakmas. Many of these tribal groups are becoming Christian. He tries to understand this phenomenon as well as evaluate the impact of this growth in Christianity upon the sociopolitical situation (1987:42-45).

CHAPTER 6

Sociopolitical and Cultural Aspects and Influences

The history of how Bangladesh was born as a nation gives special attention to the contribution of Sheikh Mujibur Rahman as the head of government. Under his leadership, the country adopted the 1972 constitution, which espoused the principles of nationalism, secularism, socialism, and democracy (Tradeport 2000:n.p.)

Politics plays a vital role in any country. The Constitution of Bangladesh has formed the basis for the nation's political organization since its adoption on November 4, 1972. Many abrupt political changes have caused suspension of the Constitution and led to amendments in almost all sections, including the total revision of some major provisions. It is notable, however, that different regimes in power since 1972 have couched major administrative changes in terms of the Constitution and attempted to legitimize changes by legally amending this basic document.

According to the Constitution, the state has a positive role to play in reorganizing society in order to create a free and equal citizenship and provide for the welfare of all. The government is required to ensure food, shelter, clothing, medical care, education, work, and social security. The government must also strengthen socialism by implementing programs to "remove social and economic inequality" and "ensure the equitable distribution of wealth among citizens" (Human Rights Internet n.d:n.p.). These far-reaching goals represented the viewpoints of many members of the 1972 Constituent Assembly. The framers of the Constitution, emerging from a period of intense repression under Pakistan, took great pains to outline the fundamental rights of citizens: all men and women are equal before the law, without discrimination based on religion, race, caste, sex, or place of birth (Human Rights Internet n.d:n.p.).

The Islamic religion was the driving force behind the creation of Pakistan and it has remained an important component of Bangladeshi ideology. The 1972 Constitution explicitly described the government of Bangladesh as secular. However, in 1977, an executive proclamation made changes in wording that did away with this legacy. Another clause stated that the government should "preserve and strengthen fraternal relations among Muslim countries based on Islamic solidarity" (Human Rights Internet n.d:n.p.). These changes in terminology reflected an overt state policy aimed at reinforcing international ties with wealthy Arab oil-producing countries. Domestically, state support for Islam, including recognition of Islam as the state religion—found in the Eighth Amendment to the Constitution written in June 1988—has not led to official persecution of other religions. Despite agitation by *Jamaat e Islami*, there was no official implementation of *sharia* or Islamic law (https://www.quora.com/Does-Bangladesh-follow-Sharia-law(accessed February 15, 2020)).

The Constitution is patterned closely on British and United States models. It established a British-style executive and a prime minister appointed from a parliamentary majority under a president. In 1975, the Fourth Amendment implemented "Mujibism" (named for Mujib), which mandates a single national party and gives the president effective authority, subject to the advice of a prime minister. Later governments of Zia and Ershad preserved the powers of the presidency and strengthened the office of the chief executive (https://biographybd.com/sheikh-mujibur-rahman/(accessed February 15, 2020)).

The rich cultural heritage of Bangladeshis seems to stem from West Bengal on the Indian side. Actually this region has a multifaceted folk heritage that was provided by the ancient Buddhist, Hindu, and Muslim roots. Bangladeshis highly value poetry, and many Bengalis consider themselves to have a poet's depth of passion and sensitivity. For example, the rebel poet, Kazi Nazrul Islam, is the national poet of Bangladesh and at heart most Bangladeshis want to be Nazrul. Another Bengali poet Rabindranath Tagore of India won the Nobel Prize for poetry in 1913. (https://www.ranker.com/list/famous-writers-from-bangladesh/reference, https://www. britannica. com/ biography/ Rabindranath-Tagore(accessed February 15, 2020)).

Arts and crafts are another aspect of culture. Culture is expressed through paintings on rickshaws and trucks. *Jamdani* was once world famous for its artistic and expensive ornamental fabric on silk and muslin. *Naksi katha*, embroidered quilted patchwork cloths produced by the village women, are familiar in both village and town. (https://ich.unesco.org/en/RL/traditional-art-of-jamdani-weaving 00879 (accessed February 15, 2020)).

Folk theatre, which is known in Bangladesh as *jatra*, is common at the village level. *Jatra* takes place usually at village fairs. Traditional Bangla music is subsumed by the cultural dominance of Indian music. Classical dancing is of various Indian schools, such as *Kathak Bharatanatyam*; indigenous folk genres are being developed. (https://www.britannica.com/place/Bangladesh/The-arts(accessed February 15, 2020)).

Language

Bengali language and script belong to the eastern most branch of the Indo-European family of languages, called Aryan or Indo-Iranian. Its direct ancestor is a form of *Prakrit* or Middle Indo-Aryan, which descended from Sanskrit or Old Indo-Aryan. Sanskrit was the spoken as well as the literary language of Aryandom until circa 500 BC. It remained the dominant literary language as well as the *lingua franca* among the cultured and erudite throughout the subcontinent for nearly two thousand years.

Bengali at the present day has two literary styles. One is *Sadhubhasa* or the literary language, and the other is *Chaltibhasa*, or the common language. The former traditional literary style is based on sixteenth-century Middle Bengali. The difference between the two literary styles is not sharp and the vocabulary is practically the same. *Sadhubhasa* has old and heavier forms while *Chalitbhasa* uses modern and lighter forms. The former shows a partiality for lexical words and compound words of the Sanskrit type, while the latter prefers colloquial words, phrases, and idioms (http://www.newworld encyclopedia.org/entry/Bengali_language(accessed February 15, 2020)).

Music

The following is a translation of the Bangladesh national anthem, "*Amar Shonar Bangla* (My Golden Bengal)," originally written by Rabindranath Tagore. It expresses the poetic nature of songs and depth of the Bengali language:

> *My Bengal of gold, I love you*
> *Forever your skies, your air set my heart in tune*
> *as if it were a flute,*
> *In Spring, Oh mother mine, the fragrance from*
> *your mango-groves makes me wild with joy-*
> *Ah, what a thrill!*
> *In Autumn, Oh mother mine,*
> *in the full-blossoms paddy fields,*
> *I have seen spread all over—sweet smiles!*
> *Ah, what a beauty, what shades, what an affection*
> *and what a tenderness!*
> *What a quilt have you spread at the feet of*
> *banyan trees and along the banks of rivers!*
> *Oh mother mine, words from your lips are like*
> *Nectar to my ears!*
> *Ah, what a thrill!*
> *If sadness, Oh mother mine, casts a gloom on your face,*
> *my eyes are filled with tears! (Bdtrade Directory n.d.:n.p.)*

Bangladeshi music has three distinct categories—classical, folk, and modern. Both vocal and instrumental classical music are rooted in the remote past of the subcontinent. Folk music is popular, nurtured through the ages by village poets and rich in devotional mysticism and love-lore. Modern Bengali music blends Western and Middle-eastern traits with traditional forms. Traditional music and songs still appeal to the public, particularly those in the rural areas.

A special genre of traditional music and songs known as *Baul* is one of the few widely-known and appreciated types of folk music in Bengal. *Baul* is not only a kind of music, it is basically a Bengali religious sect. Sect members are called *Bauls* and their songs are named for them—*baul-gan* (*baul* songs). It has been suggested that the etymology of the word derives from Sanskrit word *vatula*, which means "affected by the wind, disease, and madness." However, it might also be derived from Sanskrit word *Vyakula*, meaning "restless and disordered" (University of Maryland, Baltimore County n.d.:1).

Among the three B's of Bengali folk music—*baul, bhaoyaiya* and *bhatiyali*—*baul* is distinguished from the others textually as religious music. The texts of *bhatiyali* and *bhaiyaiya*, though they may concern Radha and Krishna, are mainly about the problems of separated lovers or unrequited love. In *baul-gan*, though songs of similar nature occur, they are thought of as allegories on the state of separation existing between the souls of men and women on spiritual grounds (Ibid.)

Musical instruments extensively used by the *bauls* are *gopiyantro, khamak, dotara, ghungur, nupur,* and *duggi. Gopiyantro*, often called *ektara*, means "one-stringed instrument" and is the most popular instrument for a *baul* singer. *Baul* singers may also use a two-stringed *dotara*. Lalon Phakir (1774-1890), a well-known exponent of *baul* music, was the most famous *baul* of all ages. He commented on the attitude of the *bauls* regarding the Hindu caste system: "What form does caste have? I have never seen it, brother, with these eyes of mine!" (Ibid.)

Drama

Drama is an old and popular tradition in Bangladesh. In Dhaka, more than a dozen theater groups have been regularly staging locally written plays as well as those adapted from famous writers, mainly of European origin. Popular theatre groups are Dhaka Theatre, *Nagarik Nattya Sampraday*, and Theatre. In Dhaka, the Baily Road area is known as *Natak Para* or Drama Village, where drama shows are regularly held. The Public Library Auditorium and Museum Auditorium are famous for holding cultural shows. Dhaka University area is a pivotal part of cultural activities (http://en.banglapedia. org/index.php?title=Theatre_Groups(accessed February 15, 2020)).

Jatra, or folk drama, is another vital expression of Bengali culture. It depicts mythological episodes of love and tragedy. Legendary plays of heroism are also popular, particularly in rural areas. In the near past, *jatra* was the biggest means of entertainment for rural Bengalis but it has declined in popularity as television, videos, and movies have become more accessible.

Dance

Dances have always been popular and prominent in Bangladesh, the chief being folk dancing. History suggests that the noted Chinese traveler, Fa-Hien, visiting Bangladesh, called it "the land of dance and music." (https://theodora.com/ encyclo-pedia/f/fahien.html(accessed February 15, 2020)). The folk dances in Bangladesh may be classified into two main groups: ritual-ceremonial and social. Ritual-ceremonial folk dances are associated primarily with seasonal customs such as harvest and religious rites that are connected closely with folk beliefs. Folk dances also project performances of certain shamans or *ojha* whose dance magic is a part of curing sick persons or ensuring the fertility of the married women. The *muharram* dance by the Muslims is ritualistic in nature. This dance accompanies stick-, sword-, or fire- dances to portray an imaginary combat with enemies. Likewise, temple dances by the Hindus are essentially religious. *Kirtana*, *baul brata*, and tribal dances are similiarly ritualistic. Besides these, certain other dances include *jari, sari, ghatu, bishahara, alkap i.* and *gambhira* (http://en.banglapedia.org/index.php?title=Folk_Dances(accessed February 15, 2020)).

Social dances possibly originated from religion but are now far removed from religious implications. Examples are the *lathi*-dance or stick-dance, boat-dance, *jatra*-dance, *baul, murshidi*, marriage dances, and the *dhali* dance. A number of social folk dances have established themselves as stage dances. In certain areas of Bangladesh, the handkerchief dance and mask dance like *chhau* dance of Purulia, West Bengal, are also prevalent. The handkerchief dance is connected with wedding festivities. *Baul* and *murshidi* dances have been greatly influenced by the dancing or whirling dervishes of the Middle East (Ibid.).

Other popular folk dances in Bangladesh are the doll-dance, *gajan* dance, *badiya* or snake charmer's dance, *charak* dance, *kathi* dance, and *leto* dance. Dance is also included in *jatra*, the popular folk play mentioned earlier. Tribal people of Chittagong, Mymensingh, Rajshahi, Dinajpur, Rangpur and Sylhet have their own typical tribal dances, too (Ibid.).

Folklore

Folklore has many forms, including myths, legends, folktales, proverbs, riddles, folk verses, folk beliefs, folk superstitions, customs, folk drama, folk song, folk music, folk dance, ballads, folk gods and goddesses, rituals, festivals, magic, witchcraft, folk art and craft, and a variety of forms of artistic expression of oral culture. Most people of rural Bengal are guided by folklore. Unfortunately, most of this is not available in written form and details may only be available in the memories of the people.

Art and Crafts

Painting in Bangladesh is a recently introduced art form. The main figure behind the art movement was Zainul Abedin, whose sketches of the Bengal famine of 1943 first attracted attention. After 1947, he gathered a school of artists around him, who experimented with various forms, both orthodox and original (*Lonely Planet* n.d.:n.p.).

Rickshaw art, on the other hand, was made to be seen "at a glance." It shows major forms of human desire such as sex, power, wealth, blessings of religious devotion, and material goods. Occasionally—especially in pieces created in 1971 at the beginnings of Bangladesh's history—they expressed the desire for a national identity. Rickshaw art images may also suggest frustrated desire, express as irony in some pictures, where animals behave like people, perhaps "saying the unsayable" politically (Kirkpatrick 1998:n.p.).

The rich and living traditions of handicrafts often transcend political boundaries that divide the people. These craft traditions are primarily folk in character; they are related closely to the area's geographic conditions and traditions of folk music, literature, and culture. The products and processes of the craftswomen and craftsmen reflect thousands of years of Bengali history, culture, and tradition. The forgotten folk gods and goddesses from the ancient past still manifest themselves in crafts made of clay, wood, brass, and other materials. Skill in the arts, however, does not replace the role of formal education in a person's life.

CHAPTER 7

Educational and Media Aspects and Influences

At the beginning of the nineteenth century, a system of liberal English-language schools based on the British model was instituted in the region that now constitutes Bangladesh. The emphasis on British education led to the growth of an elite class that provided clerical and administrative support to the colonial administration but did not develop practical skills or technical knowledge. The new elite became alienated from the masses, who had no access to the new education system (Sanisoft n.d.:n.p.).

The Pakistan period brought a general awareness of the need to restructure the education system to meet the needs of the new nation. A 1959 report by Pakistan's National Commission on Education recommended a series of reforms that would reorganize the structure of education. These reforms included emphasis on broad-based and technical education. Subsequent five-year plans and other national economic policy documents, developed during the Pakistan period, articulated the need to shift the focus of education away from rote memorization and to expand facilities for scientific and technological education. The impact of such policies was not felt in East Pakistan. With few exceptions, a liberal elite-based education system with little awareness of life in the countryside was in place when Bangladesh became independent (Bangla2000 2000:n.p.).

The main goals of the educational sector were to achieve a 70 percent literacy rate by 2002 (including among children aged six to ten) in the formal educational system and increased participation of women in literacy programs (NORAD Norwegian Agency for Development Cooperation 2002:n.p.). The latest literacy rate is 73 percent (https://knoema.com/atlas/Bangladesh/topics/Education/Literacy/Adult-literacy-rate(accessed February 15, 2020)).

Formal Education

Access to primary education in Bangladesh increased steadily from 1983 to 2003. In twenty years, enrollment figures doubled from 8.2 million to 17.6 million. The ratio of boys to girls in school narrowed from 50:1 to 40:9, and the dropout rate fell from 60 percent to 35 percent in 2000.

Cost, the main obstacle for secondary education in Bangladesh, includes tuition fees, transportation costs, purchase of uniforms, school supplies, and examination fees. The cost is so high that it is estimated to take half of a middle-income family's disposable income to support one child's education.

The Role of English and Arabic in Education

Following the birth of Bangladesh, Bangla became the sole national language and the standard language of communication. It replaced Urdu and English as the medium of instruction. The initial shortage of Bangla textbooks and other instructional materials was alleviated by the accelerated production of textbooks in the vernacular under the patronage of government education departments. The Bangla Academy also played a pioneering role in this area. In the 1980s, British education was maintained marginally through private English-language institutions attended by upper-class children. English continued to be offered as an elective subject in most institutions of higher education and was offered as a subject for bachelors and masters degrees (Government of Bangladesh 1999:1-2).

Initially, Arabic also lost prominence in independent Bangladesh. This trend ended in the late 1970s after Bangladesh strengthened its ties with Saudi Arabia and other oil-rich, Arabic-speaking countries. In the late 1980s, Arabic was studied in many Muslim homes as an integral part of religious instruction. Aside from courses in religious schools, Arabic was not a popular subject at the college and university level. An unsuccessful attempt was made in 1983 to introduce Arabic as a required language in primary and secondary levels.

Education Planning and Policy

The Fifth Five-Year Plan (1997-2002) emphasized non-formal education that sought to empower learners through literacy, numeracy, and communication skills, along with internalizing sociocultural traits. These would also affect the development of emotional and physical well-being resulting in self-actualization, expressions of creativity, and the acquisition of technological, entrepreneurial, and leadership skills. The strategies of this plan included strengthening government mass literacy centers and mobilizing NGOs and private organizations for the improvement of the overall educational system. Non-formal education was seen as complementary to the formal schooling system, through which children with no schooling and drop-outs will have access to basic education. Literacy programs could be conducted as distance learning using electronic media like radio and television (Sustainable Development Networking Programme 2001:n.p.) This is reiterated in the National Education Policy 2010 (https://educationiconnect.com/education-policy-in-bangladesh/(accessed February 15, 2020)).

Media Aspects of Bangladesh

The industrialized countries of the world use science and technology as effective tools for achieving their national objectives and changing the lifestyles of their peoples. Developing countries have fallen behind primarily because of a lack of resources and the inability to keep up with technological advances.

It is now generally realized that the inherent strength of a nation lies in skills that are acquired and enhanced through the practice of science and technology in many fields. The promotion, development, and application of scientific knowledge and technology create the necessary conditions for the socioeconomic uplift of a country. Technological progress is thus the crucial determinant in the realization of twin objectives: eradication of poverty and acceleration of socioeconomic development.

Bangladesh has struggled to meet basic needs such as food, clothing, shelter, health, and education, and to substantially raise living standards throughout the country. To achieve its national goals and keep up with the rest of the world, Bangladesh must harness science and technology. Special efforts are being made for development of information transmission media like telephone, radio, television, and internet.

Newspapers

About thirty-five daily newspapers are published in Bengali, with sixty-five online newspapers and eleven international mass media in both English and Bengali. Ninety-five percent of the population speaks Bengali and the remaining five percent speaks tribal dialects. English is spoken in some academic and business communities, especially in the cities. (bd.allmedialink.com 2018).

Radio

Radio Bangladesh and Bangladesh Television (BTV) were established in 1971 and came under state control in 1972. About 4 million radio receivers, 480,000 television sets, and 206,000 telephones were in use in 1990. Radio Bangladesh transmitted to Southeast Asia, the Middle East, Africa, and Western Europe via its shortwave station at Dhaka. Seven-and-a-half hours of daily programming were broadcast in six languages: Bangla, English, Arabic, Hindi, Urdu, and Nepali. Radio broadcast stations were reported to include 12 AM, 12 FM, and two shortwave stations as of 1999. Approximately 6.15 million people owned radios in 1997. Bangladesh Betar or Radio Bangladesh (since 1939) is operated by the government of Bangladesh with nine regional services. Other broadcasters are British Broadcasting Corporation (BBC) and Voice of America–Bengali Service.

Research findings from trends in Bangladesh media about radio shows that access to radio is through ownership and listening at a neighbor's house or a public place and, in general, is higher than access to television. In rural areas, men have more access to radios than women do. Radio is the major source of awareness-building regarding development messages like family planning, oral dehydration, and female education (http://www.mppg-nsu.org/attachments/119_final_report_faroha.pdf).

Television

The television service operates more than one hundred channels throughout the country. However, outside Dhaka the number of television sets are fewer and television is a less significant medium compared with radio, press, and word-of-mouth communications. In the countryside, broadcast communications are even less available. As of 2018, 13 percent of all rural households had radios while only 0.2 percent had televisions (CIA World FactBook:2018).

A new VHF TV network, Ekushey Television (ETV), was started to provide Bangladesh's 110 million people with a second nation-wide TV network. However, their license was revoked. The state-owned BTV network allows the reading of scriptures from the Quran, Bible, *Bhagavad-gita*, and some Buddhist meditations in its broadcasts. Also, satellite television is available with dish or cable hook for receiving channels from India and other parts of the world (Radio Netherlands Media Network, 2000:n.p.). Media in Bangladesh is only partly free: the constitution guarantees freedom of the press but media is usually monitored by the government (BBC News 2003:n.p.) This is one of the latest media policies (https://www.slideshare.net/ bnnrc/ bangladesh-national-broadcast-policy-english).

Summary

Six contextual aspects in Bangladesh influence literacy, especially its promotion. Historically, the country appreciated literacy and literary pursuits of poetry and writing, which has its impact in the arts and evolution of Bengali as a language. Religions can also promote literacy. Certainly, with the eradication of illiteracy as part of the political agenda of the ruling party, one expects increased emphasis on a better educational system. Finally, the potential influence of the media as a powerful force in transmitting information to the masses cannot be underestimated and, if harnessed well, can be used to bring Bangladesh into the twenty-first century.

CHAPTER 8

Communicatinon in Translation as used in the Bangladesh Literacy Project

Communication is a process of passing messages within a commonality among people that implies shared thoughts, space, time, language, interests, and relationships. It is one human affecting another by using various means, including verbal, written, musical, and visual, for getting a message across. All five human senses are channels that can transmit a message. Successful communication has taken place when an intended message is received. Application of communication principles to translation and to this literacy program, in particular, therefore, is important.

Communicating God's Word

The United Bible Societies (UBS) consists of 137 national Bible societies in more that 200 countries and territories (https://www.united biblesocieties.org). The mandate is to achieve the widest possible effective distribution of the Scriptures. UBS provides Scriptures in languages and media that are easily understood, faithful to the original texts in communicating the biblical message, and meet the needs of people worldwide: first, without sectarian doctrinal note or comment; and second, at a price people can afford, in a format people will receive (United Bible Societies 2000:n.p.).

Bible societies use highly qualified consultants to make the Bible available in different languages and formats. Consultants give technical support to hundreds of global translation projects. Scriptures are available digitally. They are printed in Braille for the visually impaired. For those who cannot read or prefer to listen, Scriptures are available in audio form. Bible portions or selections are produced for evangelism or Christian nurture by churches and para-church organizations. UBS translates and researches to assist Bible societies in publishing handbooks and scholarly articles. Also, they have produced Scriptures for people learning to read (United Bible Societies 2000: n.p.).

Yet the Bible societies are well aware of the gap between their ideals and the global realities (https://www.unitedbiblesocieties.org/literacy/). The UBS World Assembly, in Midrand, South Africa, in 2000 acknowledged:

> We are conscious that the context in which we are called to complete this task is a world in which around 300 million people speak languages which lack any published portions of God's Word; one half of the population is functionally non-literate; a majority of the citizens are classed by the United Nations Organization as "absolutely poor"; and millions are subject to the pressures of religious fundamentalism or tempted by the siren voices of a revived paganism. In addition, surveys reveal that many Scriptures already distributed are often inadequately used (United Bible Societies 2000:n.p.).

UBS recognized that more must be done in order to attempt to fulfill their mandate. In response, it committed to:

1. Create new products with special attention to issues and situations, available in all formats including non-print media.
2. Create products that encourage people to understand and engage personally with Scriptures.
3. Work in holistic programs, serving the whole person, recognizing the contribution of bringing the Word of Life and Hope to people in need.
4. Develop appropriate biblical materials for non-literate and new readers. (United Bible Societies 2000: n.p.)

The Meaning of Communication

Christian communication is modeled on God's communication principles as the Ultimate Communicator. God uses communication specific to a cultural context—a common space and time—so that He can be understood and draw out an appropriate response. Jesus spoke in Aramaic, the common language of the people of His day.

Sharing something in common is the basis of communication with each other (Smith 1992:24). Smith states in the summary of his Proposition one, "Communication is Involvement": "Communication is a relationship. We do not get involved in order to communicate. We communicate by being involved. Involvement is the foundation of all communication. Cultural differences only emphasize its importance" (1992:39).

Therefore, following the example set by God, Christians are commanded to communicate the good news that Christ came, died, rose again, and forgives our sins. Then, within the community of faith, we are to communicate with each other, build each other up, know, understand, and do the Word of God. Contrary to popular Christian belief, preaching is not the only means of sharing the good news. The Greek word *kerusso* from Mark 16:15b can be translated to read, "Go throughout the whole world and communicate the gospel." The message of the gospel permeates all areas of our lives, including our relationships with God, other human beings, the environment, as well as in the community in the Church (Søgaard 1993:15-18).

Many words are linked with the word *communication*, such as commune, community, and communion—words that involve relationship. Communication systems carry the messages within the relationships. It includes both processes and events. There are different circumstances in which communication takes place. The most basic, called intrapersonal communication, is within ourselves as we think through matters. Interpersonal communication can be face-to-face between two persons, in the same place at the same time, close enough to see each other clearly, or between two persons at a distance, from point to point (Søgaard 1993:31-33).

Communication dynamics change as the number of persons involved increases. Face-to-face communication can happen within a small group in a shared space and time. Likewise, there can be point-to-point small group communication as people communicate with each other at a distance. Complexity sets in as the numbers increase to large groups and then to mass communication with multiple audiences (Søgaard 1993:33-35).

Messages can be sent using signal systems. Some signal systems are spoken words, written words, numbers, pictures, sounds, body movements, objects, touch, time, space, or olfactory (which include smell and taste). Even silence communicates (Smith 1992:146). Through one or more senses, the receiver detects this signal and interprets it to give it meaning. A signal can then be sent back to the original source and the process is started all over again. This can go back and forth in a circular system.

In the midst of this interchange in the communication process, there should be some impression or impact of the message that is left with the receptor. The first stage of this impact is whether the message being sent is accepted. This is closely linked with the credibility of the messenger. Another phase of this impact is the receptor determining if the message is relevant to his or her situation; this is based on personal perception. Closely related to relevance is the specificity of the message to a personal someone and not to a general public. Often a message has an impact when it has the element of unpredictability. That the receptor was not expecting the message can cause the person consider its significance even more than normal. Finally, a message stays with a person when that person discovers for himself or herself the meaning behind the message (Kraft 1997:50).

It is important to mention the contribution of Canadian-born Herbert Marshall McLuhan (July 21, 1911-December 31, 1980). McLuhan saw changes happening from simple means of communication to technological advancement. He viewed media as "human extensions" and believed that "the print revolution" began with Gutenberg's printing press (1967:42). One unforeseen consequence of print was the fragmentation of society. McLuhan argued, "Printing, a ditto device, confirmed and extended the new visual stress. It created the portable book, which people could read in privacy and in isolation from others" (1967:50). Yet he saw electronic media as a return to collective ways of perceiving the world. His "global village" theory hinted at the ability of electronic media to unify and re-tribalize the human race (1967:52). What McLuhan did not live to see was the merging of text and electronic mass media in this new medium called the internet.

Andrew Hart (1990-1991:45) states that there are a number of basic principles that a person should understand as important characteristics of any medium:

1. The media does not reflect or replicate the world. Mediated information is, by definition, a representation or model of some part of the world and should not be accepted as being the same as "the real thing." It should not even be accepted as representing "all there is to know" about the real thing; and interaction with the model is not the same experience as interaction with the real thing. In fact, interaction with the model might be, in many instances, but a poor substitute for reality.
2. Selection, compression and elaboration occur at certain points in the complex process of editing and presenting messages. Information received through any medium, including things such as feelings evoked by pictures or sound, is no more and no less than what the sender wanted the receiver to have. This is the selection process. Actions that may have happened over a long period of time may have been compressed into a few minutes worth of reading or viewing, or a single instant may have been captured in the form of a still photograph. Students should be asking of the text "Who is communicating with whom and why; how has the text been produced and transmitted; how does it convey its meaning?"
3. Audiences are not passive and predictable but active and variable in their responses. Senders of information may think that the receivers will just accept what they are told without much further thought. However, there are many factors that can influence the receivers' perceptions of information.

4. Bearing these communication challenges and understanding in mind, the next section deals with translation as communication.

Translation as Communication

Communication principles and models can be applied to the translation of Scriptures. Translation is a form of communication. The English word "translate" comes from the Latin *translatus*, meaning "to bear, carry, bring across; to transfer" (Merriam-Webster Dictionary Online 2003:n.p.). Charles H. Kraft says, "Translation is, however, properly seen as a form of communication by means of which messages once presented in other languages in other time may come to be understood in as nearly equivalent form as possible in new languages and different times" (1997:127). In other words, a translation should not sound like a translation but as if it was originally written in the new language.

English Scriptures can be found in many versions, from the archaic English of the King James Version to modern translations. UBS favors the Good News version that emphasizes making the Scriptures readable and understandable without compromising translation standards. The same emphasis is used when translating the Scriptures into other languages as well. Another level of challenge comes when doing audio translations. In his PhD dissertation, Julian Sundersingh offers insights on how audio translations can be done. He recommends consideration of contextual issues, theoretical perspectives, biblical perspectives, text as different from hypertext; the latter is the user deciding on the entry and exit points of the text, spoken and written languages, orality, and textuality (2001:185-186).

Wayne Dye's personal relevance theory says, "People respond to the Gospel in proportion to their conviction that God and His Word are relevant to the concerns of their daily life" (1980:39). Dye's phrase, "Scripture in use," generally includes all activities intended to foster the use of scripture in the minority group we serve. . . . At the second level, the term refers to all knowledge and insights which help a translator to be most effective in fostering the use of scripture and the growth of the community of believers" (1986:3).

Another definition of "translation" is by Mildred L. Larson, who says,

> Translation ... consists of studying the lexicon, grammatical structure, communication situation, and the cultural context of the source language text, analyzing it in order to determine its meaning and the reconstructing this same meaning using the lexicon and grammatical structure which are appropriate in the receptor language and its cultural context (1984:3).

Translation of Scripture

Figure 1 helps clarify the concept of translation. It shows how a text is translated from source languages, whether it is Hebrew, Greek, or Aramaic, to a receptor language

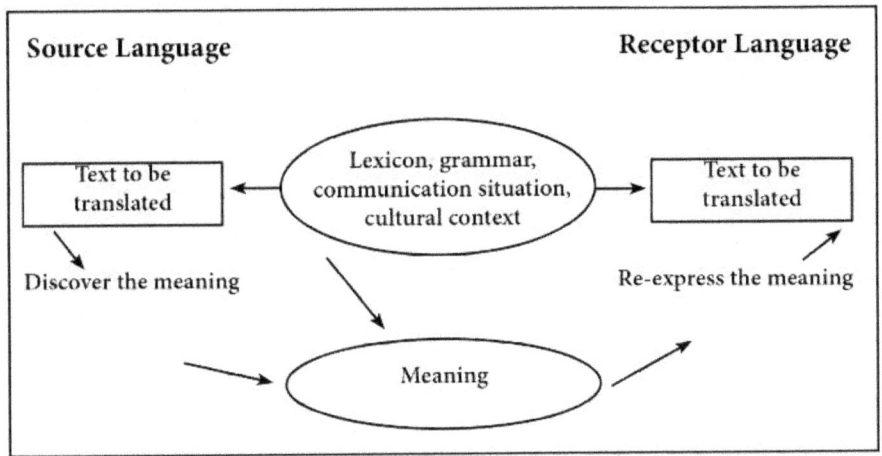

FIGURE 1: PROCESS OF TRANSLATION (Larson 1984:4)

of today. First of all, the meaning of the text must be discovered and determined by using lexicon, grammatical, communication, and cultural information, then this meaning is expressed in words of the receptor language.

R. Daniel Shaw's definition of translation reveals that "the effective repackaging of the original meaning in a form necessary to ensure the same meaning is communicated with more or less the same impact for those who now receive it for the first time" (1987:2). It is to ensure the "common message experience" as seen in Figure 2.

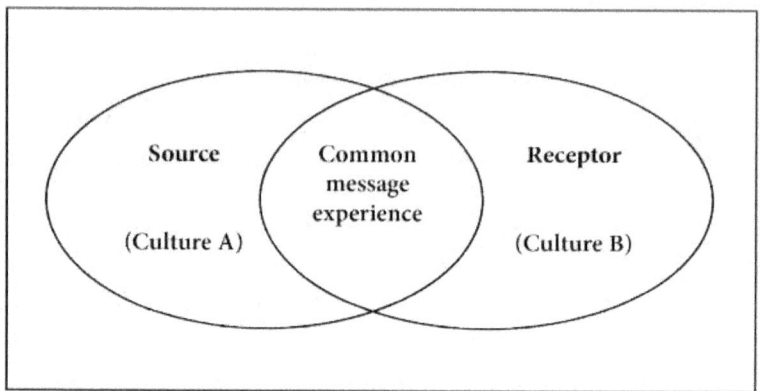

FIGURE 2: SOURCE, MEANING, AND RECEPTOR MODEL OF COMMUNICATION (Shaw 1987:18)

The process of transferring the message in a source language to a receptor language involves two cultures. The translator brings his or her experiences to the communication process and should also consider the translation context, the source culture, and even his or her own cultural bias. The receptor's culture interacts with the process of translation and brings about adequate and meaningful translation.

Audio Translations

As Bible translators consider the area of translating for the audio medium, there are a number of new considerations. It is important when doing direct speech to consider the mood of the original speaker. Was she happy or sad, angry or glad? In some cases, there is implied information that it is assumed that the reader should know. When reading the Scriptures, it is important to consider the question, "Where does the reader for audio place emphasis in the sentences?" Expressions like surprise, sadness, or anger must be communicated. Bridge material "that links the gaps in Scripture material" is needed. The following is adapted from Søgaard, who points out the complexity of translation is the challenge of translating from an ancient time and a culture often far removed from modern settings. He lists the implications of the oral characteristics of Scriptures for audio programs (2001:26-2):

1. Direct versus indirect speech. This concern recognizes that the original speaker was speaking or his or her speech was being reported. This would determine if a character voice should be used or a narration.
2. Implicit information. This would include names of people, places, and events. In the literacy materials used in Bangladesh, the term "Jews" had to be explained. A short introduction of Luke as a doctor was also made as a prelude to presenting selected verses on the Life of Christ from the Gospel of Luke. Sometimes Jewish feasts were explained before a passage that referred to that festival was read.
3. Emphasis. This refers to determining which is the most important part or word of the verse, where the emphasis should be placed. As a verse is read, if the emphasis is placed at the wrong word, it can take on a totally different meaning. In John 3:16, the emphasis could be placed on a variety of words or phrases, "For God so loved the world that he gave his only begotten son that whosoever believes in him shall be saved." If we try putting emphasis on different words and phrases we will see how this changes the meaning. Sometimes it is important to refer back to the original language and other times it is important to weigh the theological significance. In the case of John 3:16 the emphasis on God reflects the crux of the matter, that God initiated salvation for humankind.
4. Expression. Tone of voice carries the mood of the moment. The mood of the speaker is conveyed by how the speech is made, whether in anger or in a pastoral manner.

Receptor Language Framework

Translators are the immediate source of translations, which means that they are both receptor and source. They are secondary receptors unless they participate in an original communication called simultaneous interpreting, speak the receptor language as their mother tongue, and have an adequate comprehension of source language. The source language and cultural context may be learned through the medium of a world language, which may or may not be the translator's own. Attitudes of translators towards the receptor language and source language are important. For example, if they love Greek and Hebrew more than the receptor's language, they may be tempted to carry over the foreign forms. On the other side, translators who are enamored by receptor language want to keep out the foreign or preserve exotic differences and incorporate into the Scriptures. Translators need to be objective and sufficiently informed of literary potentials of receptor language (Nida and Reyburn 1981:20-21).

Translators need to think about the message in terms of the receptor-language framework based on pre-suppositions and values of the culture, while keeping the tension between knowing the language-context of the source language and the average receptor frame of interpretation in their own culture. Translators recognize the disparity between the source and receptor languages and the corresponding presuppositions and values. An effort is made to balance out these crucial difficulties. However, a correction may introduce foreign terms and subsequent errors in transitioning the content from the source language to the receptor language as Figure 3 illustrates the complexity of the translation process (Nida and Reyburn 1981:21-22).

Using borrowed terms can be legitimate but filling them with the true content is no easy task. Descriptive phrases are much better than borrowed foreign terms. Western Christianity has mainly used the verbal and written channels of communication to teach religion. However, people may know a lot about God without believing; they have cognitive knowledge but no faith (Nida and Reyburn 1981:23).

Scriptures preserved the witness of a believing community in an oral form as written texts were too expensive. Today, the Bible is available in inexpensive formats and can also be distributed freely. Some want the Bible to have background information useful to present-day readers. Others want a translation that is rewritten to contain the same truths in a new cultural setting. The latter view is rejected as the historical setting is regarded as highly important to the integrity of the documents themselves. Background information can help the reader, but if commentary is added to the text, it ceases to be a translation (Nida and Reyburn 1981:23-24).

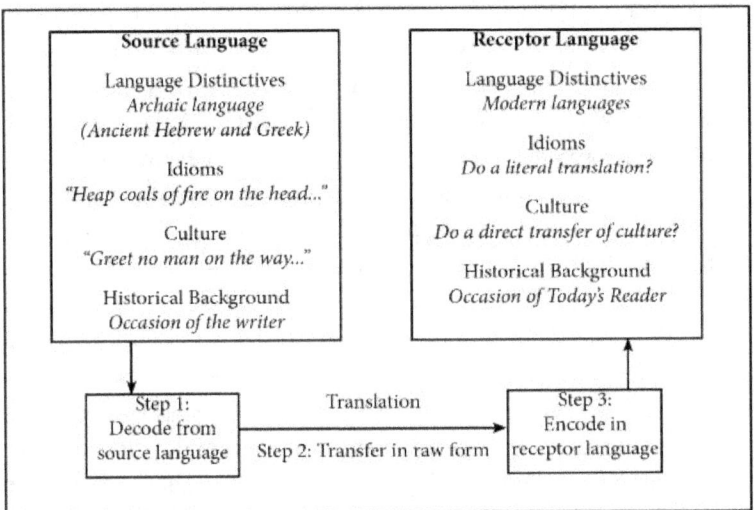

FIGURE 3: TRANSLATION PROCESS (Martin n.d:n.p.)

Translators seek to minimize misunderstanding of the text but there are limitations to this goal. Sensitive translators recognize that many accounts in the Scriptures can be misunderstood. However, readers do not seem unduly disturbed by what they do not understand or by what they judge as contradictory or inconsistent. Mainly, they conclude that it is their own problem of comprehension. A translator can provide only a limited amount of adjustment and supplementary information. A translation is not a substitute for a commentary, sermon, or teaching.

Differences of presuppositions exist within a single society, yet there is also commonality among cultures that makes translation possible:

> In a sense the Bible is the most translatable religious book that has ever been written, for it comes from a particular time and place . . . through which passed more cultural patterns and

out from which radiate more distinctive features and values than has been the case with any other place in the history of the world. If one were to make a comparison of the culture traits of the Bible with those of all existing cultures today . . . one would find that in certain respects the Bible is surprisingly closer to many of them than to the technological culture of the western world. It is this "western" culture that is the aberrant one in the world. And it is precisely in the western world, and in the growing number of persons in other parts of the world who share its worldview, that the Scriptures have seemingly the least ready acceptance (Nida and Reyburn 1981:28).

Universal needs from real life are portrayed in Scripture, making the Bible appealing in many societies. The Bible is concerned with God's activity in human history. Exegesis is the process of reconstructing the communication event by determining its meanings. Hermeneutics, on the other hand, points out parallels between the biblical relevance and appropriate response for the believer. Both fall under the category of interpretation. Hermeneutics depends on linguistic and cultural transpositions, whereas exegesis provides historical accuracy and a meaningful basis for later exposition. Translators should provide the closest natural equivalent of the source-language message so that it may be used by receptor-language expositors in their task of transposition (Nida and Reyburn 1981:32).

CHAPTER 9

Using Media to Communicate Scriptures

Scriptures are increasingly offered through media. It is vital even in non-literate or semi-literate cultures.

Foundational Studies for Using Media

Hodgson and Soukup edited sixteen papers, which were originally presented at an American Bible Society (ABS) sponsored academic symposium, "From One Medium to Another," held in New York in September 1995 (http://1981.catholic-resources.org/Bible/Review_Hodgson-Soukup.htm). The symposium focused on a broad use of the word "translation" and asked, "How can the message of the Holy Scriptures be faithfully translated and communicated from one medium to another?" These articles address the present-day possibilities of translating Scriptures in various non-print media. Unfortunately, as reviewed by Felix Just, "Given the realities of international politics and economics . . . such predictions are overly optimistic, ignoring the likelihood that many poor people will not have access to such technologies for a long time to come" (2000:78-80).

An article by Cherie Tellier (n.d.:n.p.) emphasized the importance of the Bible regardless of the medium in which it is presented. The Bible serves as a tangible means of communicating with God, in which it transmits stories and information so that meaning can be carried from one generation to the next. Christians throughout the centuries have used the Bible for preaching, teaching, worshipping, and telling their faith. Scriptures have shifted back and forth from oral to written tradition and now to non-print media.

Plato commented on the negative impact of the written word. He believed that writing destroys one's memory and that the written text is unresponsive and cannot defend itself as the spoken word can (Ong 1982:79). In a world that is technologized, the written word now can again be communicated in a more dynamic, interactive way and the Bible will survive—no matter the medium in which it is presented.

Considerations for Multi-Media Literacy Program Design

When using non-print media to communicate meaning, sensitivity to the audience or receptor-orientation is of utmost importance. It is the responsibility of the communicator or translator to be well-versed in the particular needs of their target audience and to understand the ways in which the audience participates in giving meaning to the texts being communicated. Communicators or translators are to assume that the audience has no familiarity with church language or traditional Bible terminology, they have limited Bible knowledge and limited reading skills, and their primary contact with biblical text is through hearing it read aloud or quoted in some form.

In relation to this literacy project, it was important to single out the audio component as a non-print medium and highlight its unique features. The following points are adapted from Søgaard (1993:160-166):

1. Sound is the main medium of communication. A person who is not deaf can hear. One can listen as one is doing other tasks even. There can be more than one audience listening. As in the case of the literacy project, there were secondary listeners who were either gaining Bible knowledge or information even though they were not formally in the literacy class. They may not be able to read and write but they are able to listen and remember.
2. As already indicated, the user decides how, when, and where to use the audio component. Since men and women in the villages of Bangladesh each had their own routine, it was not uncommon to have the literacy groups scheduled for different times. The women preferred day gatherings just

after cooking one meal and before starting the next. The men, who usually worked until dusk, preferred meeting at night after they had their meal and were relaxing. This meant that their classes could be from 8-10 p.m. or 9-11 p.m.
3. For the program, each literacy center, which consisted of both men's and women's groups, shared the resource of a listening device. However, it was not uncommon for at least one group member to own their own personal device. These would borrow the audio materials and play them for themselves and others to hear outside of class times.
4. These devices cost less than televisions and video players. Production costs of an audio product also tend to be lower than the other productions such as video.
5. An audio product is small, does not require high maintenance, and the length of listening time is flexible.
6. The devices are relatively simple to operate and maintain in good condition. Participants were instructed on how to use the device and can operate it.
7. These audio products can be taken and used virtually anywhere. Classes were often conducted in the open air or in someone's cowshed.
8. They offer flexible opportunities for access as they can be listened to at any time unlike a radio program that must be listened to at a particular time. Usually the class chose to start to listen from wherever they wanted to listen to but they were also able to cue it to the place they wanted to listen to again like the joint letter words or even to sing along with the songs.
9. Keeping the sequence is particularly important. When listening to a series in a program, these products made sure that the sequence is not lost. All the products were carefully numbered and labeled both on the box and on its label. As a group, all the participants were at the same place of learning and so it was not a problem to follow in sequence.
10. This product may be listened to repeatedly. Each group listened to it no less than seven times. This re-emphasized and reminded them of the lesson.

11. Listening to this product was effortless as compared to attending a lecture. A person can relax and listen.
12. The ability to listen in private helps overcome the barriers of embarrassment. The materials were designed for both group and personal use.
13. Audience segmentation is possible. These programs can be geared towards specific audiences. The language for a second edition of the literacy materials was changed to suit a Muslim audience.
14. Local art forms can be employed. Programming on the audio product can use local talents, music, language, and cultural forms of communication. Dialects are commonly used for local color.
15. The product can be used to teach new songs and otherwise be used to share other aspects of education. These audio products were designed for teaching literacy which passed literacy standards and techniques.

The literacy materials developed by the BBS have blended the use of audio and print. The curriculum is receptor-oriented and need-based, which has captured the interest of the participants. This multimedia and multi-sensory approach has maintained high motivation among those who have chosen to join the literacy groups using the Bible Society materials. An excellent, yet inexpensive and small, medium of an audio product has been used.

A Comprehensive Communication Model

Application of communication theories can be explained by the use of appropriate models. Communication models can be helpful in illustrating the communication process showing the connectivity and relationship of each component to each other. A word of caution, however, is that no model is perfect. No model takes into consideration all the possible variables and their relationship to the communication process. Do not confuse models with the real situation.

The communication process is complex, but considering what happens with each element eases the complexity. The comprehensive model illustrated in Figure 4 includes all the elements of the communication process. They are numbered in the order in which the process takes place but placed closest to the other elements it relates to. Lines and arrows also join related elements and indicate how the process flows.

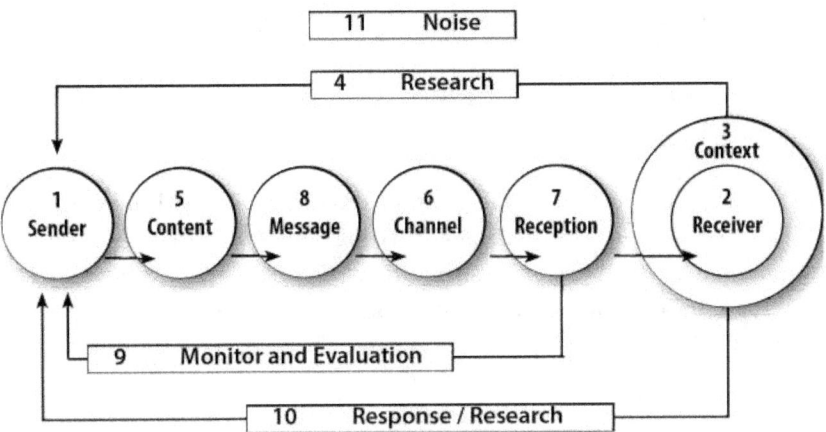

FIGURE 4: COMPREHENSIVE COMMUNICATION PROCESS
(Søgaard 1993:51)

The elements in the communication process include (Søgaard 1993:47-51):

- Sender: Christian communicators engaged in persuasive communication.
- Receiver: the audience to whom the communication is directed.
- Context: location and environment of the audience.
- Research: gathering information needed on audience and context of audience.
- Content: Scriptures to be selected that address the needs of the audience.
- Channel: communication approach and medium to carry content.

- Reception: ensuring that the audience will receive the content by being culturally sensitive.
- Message: the program format that depends on the media chosen.
- Monitoring and evaluating: monitoring all aspects in the process and careful evaluating of the program.
- Response and research: feedback and measuring of actual results.
- "Noise": any aspect, permeates all parts that tries to hinder good communication.

In the last section of this chapter these elements will be used to describe the context in Bangladesh. Using Søgaard's categories in his comprehensive communication model (1993:47-51), the following is useful in framing the context in Bangladesh.

Sender

In the Bangladesh context, the BBS along with different local churches are the senders. Their primary concern is to send the good news of Jesus Christ so that it is heard and understood by Bengali people in meaningful ways that touch their lives.

In order for the message to be received and accepted, the senders need to establish credibility with the audience. The BBS is an officially registered non-profit organization with the government of Bangladesh under the Society Act. On the local level, the BBS is in good standing with local Protestant denominations, as well as the Roman Catholic Church. Most churches depend on the BBS for supplies of Bibles, Scripture portions, tracts, and audio products. It is important to uphold and maintain the integrity of the Bible Society to churches and secular leadership, as well as to the public at large, in order to be accepted as a sender that can be trusted.

Receiver

It is important to describe the audience that this literacy program is directed to: who they are, what their needs are, what age group they are in, and what other categories they are in. In the case of a literacy program in Bangladesh, the receivers would primarily be new readers in the rural village setting of Bangladesh. Farmers, farmers' wives, and school dropouts may join this program because they had been a part of a basic literacy program before and want to improve their literacy skills to a functional level. The ideal age group would be no younger than fifteen years old and not older than forty as these would be the ones who could be most receptive. Due to the scope of a literacy program, it should be open to all people: Christians, Hindus, animists, and Muslims.

Location Context

The location context in Bangladesh is primarily rural and includes the districts of Rangpur, Rajshahi, Mymensingh, and, in the south of Dhaka—Barisal. BBS and local churches have literacy groups in these places.

The environments of the receivers are their villages, sitting on the ground, reading by the light of a lamp after a hard day's work. If the receivers are Hindus, animists, or Muslims, they may be in the literacy group out of curiosity. Some in the villages may be hostile towards the people and the program.

Research

Research of the receiver and the location context is important and is the foundation for engagement of any media production. The findings from research can indicate the needs of the receivers. It can determine the opinions of the audience. Information is needed in order to feed effective materials into production.

Research can be conducted in both formal and informal ways. Formal research can be quantitative, such as surveys, and qualitative, such as interviews and focus groups. A personal example of informal research is the occasion on which I did farm work for one day. The purpose of this was so that I could understand how a farmer feels after a day of hard work. At the end of that day of working in the fields harvesting, bundling, pounding, and sifting rice, I was tired. After this experience, I concluded that a farmer had to be highly motivated to sit on the ground to learn to read after a hard day's work.

Content

Selection of the content of the literacy program should be Scripture passages that address the needs of the audience. It would be important to develop themes that were contemporary and relevant to the villagers of Bangladesh. Using drama, local music, Bengali folk tunes and styles, such as Scripture-in-song, would be necessary to attract the audience. Reading Scriptures clearly and explaining difficult words would help give the background to Bible stories.

Another interesting development in selecting content was a meeting with some church leaders of the Lutheran church, who said that many village pastors were new readers and had little Bible knowledge. These pastors indicated a need to develop materials for village pastors and Christians for the purpose of increasing Bible reading, knowledge, and strengthening discipleship. They wanted these specialized literacy materials to cover the life of Christ, Old Testament characters, New Testament letters, and Christian practices.

Channel

Many good methods can be used to communicate to an audience. However, the question of which one would fit best with each given situation has to be answered. A helpful criteria grid to determine this would be content, context, and available resources. For example, if the content needed to be transmitted through an auditory medium, then audio products or the radio would be most appropriate. The context further defines which technology would be appropriate. In a primarily Islamic country, such as Bangladesh, it is difficult for a Christian organization to get radio time. In addition, radio as a medium may not be as versatile as an audio product. For resources, it may be possible to get a grant to supply devices and batteries for literacy groups where ten to twenty people can share them.

Reception

To ensure that the message is received with a common message experience, it is important that the message is presented in a Bengali way in the Bangladeshi context. Søgaard says, "Here we are concerned with exposure to the message, captivating attention of the audience, gaining understanding, and commitment to retention and action" (1993:49).

Literacy may be a good way for Hindus, animists, and Muslims to be exposed to stories told by Jesus. It can captivate the imagination because the materials offer practical solutions to their felt needs and also address their real spiritual needs. An audio product would serve to give explanations to difficult concepts or communicate the needed background information orally. Retention and action would be encouraged as these materials call for practical application.

Message or Program Format

The message or program format is heavily dependent on which medium of communication is chosen. With an audio product, great emphasis is placed on how a program should sound. In addition, in terms of audience reception of the program, a simple program format would be helpful as villagers are limited to their immediate setting. Since the program has a goal of literacy, it would be produced as an educational tape, with "teachers" who spoke to the listeners. Attention would be given to practical matters such as announcing a particular page to turn to or a related exercise to complete.

Program format would include getting and maintaining the audience's attention and illustrating the text's application through a drama with local flavor. Reading Scripture is a goal of the program, so the speed at which it is read should be neither too fast nor too slow, with careful pronunciation. Helping the new reader to recognize words would be important because Bengali words with combination-letters are common and difficult.

Songs, such as a Scripture-in-song, could reinforce the Scripture text. Using well-known tunes could make the songs familiar to the listener.

Monitoring and Evaluating

Monitoring and evaluating should be built in to any program from the beginning. Materials should go through pre-testing, testing, and re-working. Only then should materials be produced—in limited quantity. To do product research, basic recordings and mock-ups of materials should be created. The target audience should be asked to listen, touch, see, and use the materials. The audience's opinions are important: did they like or dislike the material—and why? How could the product be improved?

For longer term monitoring and evaluating, careful records should be kept on the number of participants, as well as when, where, and how the program is conducted. With a goal of gauging the impact on literacy, valuations should be done on each person's level of reading, comprehension, and writing at the beginning and at the end of the program. For monitoring purposes, periodic reading and comprehension evaluations would be done throughout the program.

Response and Research

It is important to design research to measure the effects of the program. Both the positive and negative effects should be reported. In addition to knowing that a program is working, it is vital to know how it is working.

Feedback should be through the network of all those involved in a literacy program. The main sources of information and feedback come from actual participants. The next source could be the facilitators who coordinate literacy groups. Another level would be reports on progress from supervisors and coordinators, including project challenges such as breakdowns in the audio devices or batteries. Information can also be gathered from church and local leaders who see whether the program has had any impact on the church or on the village life as a whole.

Noise

"Interfering with the messages is noise, which is anything that distorts the message intended by the source, anything that interferes with the receiver's receiving the message as the source intended the message to be received" (Society for Technical Communication 2002:n.p.). The issue of noise is ever present and permeates the whole communication process in this literacy program. Potential sources of noise are numerous.

One source is culture. Components that are not culturally sensitive, not using the Bengali language, and not referring to local customs and practices, will create noise in the minds of the listeners. Another source of noise may be theology. The theologies of the Christian, Muslim, and Hindu listeners are quite different. The differences between the religious groups may be as basic as monotheism versus polytheism. Even among Christians, denominational biases may create some theological questions.

There is also noise from personal sources. These are as unique and as varied as each individual listener. People prefer different learning styles: visual, auditory, by doing written exercises, by verbalizing, and alone versus in a group. Any combination of these may become educational noise. Educational backgrounds may differ: some participants enter the program with formal education, while those who have been self-taught may begin on the other end of the educational spectrum. Age-based noise can occur because younger people learn differently from older people in terms of speed, understanding, and ways of responding. Gender-based noise may come from men and women learning and interacting in different ways.

Ecclesiastical noise may result from the church not having a good reputation in the community or being known as a place to receive benefits such as free food, material things, and education. The noise created here could hinder reception of the biblical message and literacy training, which are the main goals. Media noise could happen when the media chosen is not the choice of the people who may prefer visual media like television or video.

Summary

Communication is important in translation and media, particularly as they are applied to this literacy program. The mandate of UBS is to communicate the Scriptures. It seeks to provide Scriptures that are faithful to the source language, in easily-understood common languages, and in a media format that meets the need of the people. UBS products are not to include any sectarian doctrinal note or comment. It needs to be affordable as well.

At the UBS World Assembly in South Africa in 2000, the participants articulated the reality that many languages do not have any published Scriptures. Half of the world's population is functionally non-literate. There is rampant, abject poverty, a resurgence of fundamental religions, and a revival of many beliefs. Bible societies also recognized that many of the Scriptures distributed were not effectively used. In response, the UBS must create products that address these challenges.

An adequate understanding of communication is necessary to use media effectively to communicate the Scriptures. Communication leads to relationships in a process of events. There are different methods in which we communicate with ourselves and expand communication with others. The dynamics of communication are complicated by adding more participants, geographical distance, and various signal systems.

McLuhan viewed media as extensions of a human being (McLuhan 1967:1). His critique of the print media is that it causes people to disconnect from each other. However, he saw that media could create a global village. His prediction became a reality with the internet.

Any model represents part of the world and is not to be accepted as the only reality. Most media projection is selective, compressed, and elaborates a biased point of view. It is important to ask who is communicating with whom and why. Also, audiences have minds of their own and are influenced by factors in their context.

Translation involves communicating from a source language to receptor language. The process of translation is an art that, when done well, will result in a product that is so natural that it will not seem foreign. The complexity of translation is experienced from one medium to another.

The Bible will survive regardless of its medium. However, an audio format returns it to an oral tradition similar to the Bible's source culture and language. Therefore, using audio products has great advantages.

Søgaard's comprehensive model was used as a framework to understand this literacy program. It outlined the ingredients that make up this program from the sender-receiver to the potential noise sources.

CHAPTER 10

The Experimental Literacy Project in Bangladesh

Based on the context, principles, and communication insights in previous chapters, a literacy project was developed in Bangladesh. In the early 1980s, the BLM-D started literacy groups of economically poor village folk who eagerly sat together by the light of dim kerosene lamps learning to read. In the following years many groups completed one year of basic literacy training. At least 1,250 persons completed these basic literacy courses. BLM-D felt a need to study how many of these "graduates" continued using their literacy skills. This mission also worked with a local denomination, Bangladesh Lutheran Church (Schrøder 1993:4).

At the same time, the UBS was interested in knowing the results of the use of the six booklets that had been translated into Bengali in the NRP. Since no study had been done, there was no evidence whether new readers could actually read these booklets. The UBS also desired to experiment with new approaches to literacy training with audio-based Scriptures.

In 1990, UBS commissioned the author to do a baseline research study to determine how many who completed their literacy program were still using their literacy skills and if they could read the NRP. This baseline study showed that approximately ten percent of the graduates retained their reading skills one year after completing the course. It also showed that the NRP materials were too difficult to read (Chai 1990:3).

In that survey, the target audience was asked about the possibility of using audio products. The response was positive. Perhaps this low literacy could be overcome by developing cassette audio products that would go along with the Bible stories in order to help new readers read and familiarize themselves with the words. The audio medium would motivate the participants' interest. The learning system would build on a sound-word recognition, bearing in mind that adults learn differently from children. The materials would be graduated for beginner, intermediate, and advanced reading levels.

UBS developed literacy materials after a period of product testing, bridging basic literacy and functional literacy with NRP in literacy training using audio products. Eventually two different tracks of materials were developed. The first was general training towards functional literacy for anyone who wanted to participate regardless of religion. The second track would be for both literacy training and discipleship Christians. The first track was called "Good News" or *Shukhobor* and the second track was "Path of Salvation" or *Muktir Path*.

Shukhobor—Materials for New Readers in Villages

Both tracks were geared towards those who had completed a basic literacy course. They knew the letters of the alphabet, could read and write simple sentences, and perhaps could do some math. The first track, *Shukhobor*, used principles of primer development. The basic philosophy behind the teaching-learning approach emphasized consistent teaching, with the addition of the audio products. It was possible to do self-study as the materials were self-contained. In a culture that enjoys being in a group, there were interactive dynamics in these literacy groups. Facilitators formed and maintained the groups. The group members read and wrote in the primers.

There were three sets for general new readers in villages:

- Set 1, "Good News for a Friend," was the primary set, which builds up from a basic ability to read. It helps a new reader with combined letters. The stories are in simple Bengali.
- Set 2, "Good News for the Family," was an intermediate set, which tackles issues facing the family in the village. This is for those who have completed Set 1.
- Set 3, "Good News for the Farmer," was the advanced set having many agricultural stories.

TABLE 5: MATERIALS SUMMARY OF *SHUKHBOR*

Name of Set	Number of audio products	Print support
Set 1, "Good News for a Friend"	4	4 primers 6 NRP booklets
Set 2 "Good News for the Family"	4	4 primers 1 Life of Christ booklet
Set 3 "Good News for the Farmer"	4	1 New Testament Common Language
Entire *Shukhobor* Track	12	6 NRP booklets 8 primers 1 Life of Christ booklet 1 New Testament Common Language

The three parts move the learner from beginner literacy to intermediate literacy to functional literacy. There were four audio products and four primers in each set. The pictures on the cassette and book covers suit the theme. On the audio products were two "guides" who helped the listener through the tape, teaching and reading the stories. On each side of these audio products were Bible stories taken from the NRP. The combined-letter words were spelled out and difficult words were explained. Two special features were a drama and a song on each side of the tape. See Table 5 for a summary of *Shukhobor*.

Muktir Path—Material for New Readers in the Church

This second track of materials was developed concurrently with *Shukhobor*, maintaining the concept that the materials were written for new readers who are at a functional literacy level. The target audience was Christians converts from Hinduism who have had little discipleship. The purpose was to help the person have an overall understanding of the Bible. The self-contained feature of these materials were helpful for church leaders who may want to improve their literacy skills in private.

This track had four sets: Set 1, "The Path of Salvation, Luke's Gospel," Set 2, "The Path of Salvation, Old Testament Passages," Set 3, "The Path of Salvation, Living Letters," and Set 4, "Path of Salvation, Faith-Building Topics." The first set used exactly 336 verses or about forty percent of the Gospel of Luke to present a comprehensive picture of the life of Christ. The second set reflects the need for Christians to know the Old Testament. Until 2000, the whole Bible was not translated in the common language. Therefore, Christian new readers could not read the Old Testament for themselves. (The Carey Bible was written in difficult-to-read literary Bengali.) An understanding of the Old Testament is needed in order to make sense of the New Testament, such as references to characters found in the Old. Each of the six tapes used Old Testament passages in chronological order to tell life stories of major Old Testament characters, such as Adam, Moses, and David. The third set introduced the many letters written to advise and encourage believers in the Early Church and the Church today. The epistles that were used in the literary program were presented in the order found in the New Testament. The verses selected gave the main message of the letter. The fourth set used certain topics that are mentioned repeatedly in the Bible. These topics are important to the Christian faith for spiritual growth (see Table 6).

TABLE 6: MATERIALS SUMMARY OF *MUKTIR PATH*

Name of Set	Number of Audio Products	Print Support
Set 1 "Life of Christ"	4	Gospel of Luke
Set 2 "Twelve prominent characters of Old Testament"	6	Old Testament in Common Language
Set 3 "Understanding the New Testament (Acts to Revelation)"	6	New Testament in Common Language
Set 4 "Relevant topics from Bible"	6	Bible in Common Language
Entire Muktir Path Track	22	Gospel of Luke New Testament Bible

Developmental Concepts for Both Tracks of Materials

The challenge was to teach literacy using proven and effective techniques, meeting literacy standards with carefully considered materials, combined with the use of audio products. These audio products essentially became the "teacher." The materials were graded from easy, intermediate, and advanced. The goal was functional literacy for the UBS's goal of being able to read the Common Language Bible. The Bible stories were central in addressing a particular need of the audience such as savings, relationships, and farming. For example, in the parable of the sower, in Luke 8, the scattering of seeds is exactly the way a Bangladeshi farmers sow seeds. These stories were found in the NRP and the Common Language New Testament.

Those in the program would hear the audio products as the primary audience, with the secondary audience of bystanders who often listened in as the groups meet outdoors in the village. Although they could not read, they could gain knowledge by listening in to the content.

Literacy primers included the Scripture passages, word explanations, and written exercises. The audio products used the familiar spoken language. The basic package was envisioned as a self-contained self-study or a group study.

The second track of materials was developed for use in churches by Christian new readers. BLC church leaders expressed the need for materials for village pastors and church members who were new readers. Many villagers did not know much of the life of Christ, Old Testament characters and stories, and New Testament letters, and had no teaching on basic Christian topics such as giving. The BBS already had a printed booklet entitled "The Man Who Gave His Life," which was the gospel of Luke, so this was used as the reader for the first set of materials. With the help and approval of Kenneth Thomas, a UBS Translation Consultant, the 336 verses from the Gospel of Luke mentioned gave a broad sweep and complete overview of the life of Christ.

A few months later, twenty BLC leaders attended a workshop on script-writing. Participants struggled with the passages in Luke to make up Scripture-in-songs, dramas, and scripts. Although the efforts did not result immediately in a complete set of materials, it was a meeting where ideas were germinated. The BLC leaders established ownership of this track and named the materials *Muktir Path*, the Path of Salvation.

Bengali

The Bengali language is complex and so translation is challenging. The fifty-two letters in the Bengali alphabet can combine to form a combined-letter that takes a different look from that of the original two letters. When used, this becomes a combined-letter word. The changes make the new letter look quite different from the original letters, as seen after the equal sign (Figure 5).

Letter A	Letter B	Combination-letter	As used in a word
দ	ধ	দ্ধ	বুদ্ধিমান
স	স্ট	স্ট	বৃষ্টি
ন	ত	ন্ত	কিন্তু

FIGURE 5: BENGALI COMBINED LETTERS

The first line has the Bengali letters translated as d and dh that become the combined letter ddh. The combined-letter word is *buddhiman* which means "wiseman." The letters in the second line are S and St becoming SSt. The word is *brissti* meaning "rain." The third set of letters is n and t combining to nt. The word formed is *kintu*, meaning "but."

Another complication is that there are different types of Bengali. Standard Bengali, taught in books, has Sanskrit roots and therefore has more terms from traditional "Hindu." *Muslimani* Bengali has more Arabic terms imported to the Bengali language. For example, different Bengali words are used to refer to God such as *Koda* and *Allah*, instead of the Sanskrit word *Issore*. Dialects in Bengali can be found according to the districts and villages. For example, in Sylhet and Chittagong, the dialect sounds like a different language and cannot be understood easily by Bengalis from other parts of Bangladesh. Calcutta Bengali is similar to standard Bengali but those from India think that they have a purer form that is considered high, classical, or literary Bengali. These different types of the Bengali make teaching the language, as well as using print and audio together, complex.

Working Group

A working group was formed to create these materials. The function of this team was to brainstorm on the themes and actually write some prototype materials for pre-testing. As such, there had to be a combination of knowledge, skills, experience, and talents.

I led the working group, due to my experience in cross-cultural communication, research, and six years of work in church ministries and missions. Richmond Joydhor, the Media Officer for the BBS, was a poet and song-writer, with experience in audio production. George Munshi was a literacy consultant in an organization funded by World Council of Churches called Council of Churches Development of Bangladesh. He had met the famous Frank Laubach who had come to Bangladesh. Munshi had written literacy primers using the Laubach method. P. Halder was a retired headmaster and lay pastor for the Bangladesh Baptist *Songgo* (Church). He had been translating from English to Bengali for the Bible Society. He was also on the BBS Board and Media Committee. Consultancy and training was provided by Viggo Søgaard and Julian Sundersingh, UBS Media Consultants, and experts in communication and the use of media.

The working group decided to choose stories from the NRP as these were the materials that the BBS had already developed for new readers. The first stories chosen were the wise and foolish builders (Luke 6:46-49) and the widow's offering (Mark 12:41-44). The village people could identify with these stories, which were culturally appropriate. The floods in the story of the wise and foolish builders were a familiar natural disaster in Bangladesh, and the presence of poor widows in the village was common.

The working group analyzed the words used in these stories. Combined-letters and difficult words were isolated and compiled in word-lists that were then explained. Vocabulary was limited, along with a conscientious effort to use simple everyday words. It was ensured that the grammar was not difficult and that the sentences were not too long. The words were carefully chosen with explanations for the beginner level of the new reader. The materials were developed with attention to a conscious gradation of difficulty from beginner to intermediate to advanced. The font size, a little larger than the regular font, had a clear, simple, rounded appearance.

Members of the working group devised and wrote exercises, which were mainly comprehension questions that went along with the stories. There were also math exercises because some of the stories dealt with numbers. The answers, found at the back of the primers, were printed upside down so that the new reader would complete the exercises before checking for the correct answer. There was careful coordination between written text and audio product with the cassette taking the lead. The user was guided through the materials in the primers as page numbers were announced on the audio products.

Script-Writing and Primer-Writing Workshops

Script-writing and primer-writing workshops were conducted to create materials suited for the context. Workshop participants included local script-writers, song-composers, educators, and new readers representing the target audience. These training workshops began with an explanation of the mission statement of the literacy program. This ensured that those who worked on the materials understood the purpose of the materials and the need to simplify the language to the level of the target audience. Writers were also required to be respectful, not talking to new readers in a condescending way as if they were children or unintelligent. The materials had to be both educational and entertaining to keep readers motivated.

One format was a taped program with two narrators, a woman and a man, who would dialogue with each other. They referred often to the listener as if he or she were there with them. The two narrators would encourage the listener along in the learning process. Another taped format used a teacher and a new reader conversing together.

Workshop participants worked on:

- themes for each lesson, such as saving money.
- Scripture selections that would be appropriate for each theme.
- background necessary to understand Scriptures selected.
- narration for the scripts to make the program flow.
- dramas appropriate to the themes that illustrated life situations.
- songs based on Scripture passages.
- word lists of difficult words found in the text and explained in the primers.
- exercises for primers based on the stories and theme.

Table 7 gives an example of the final program format. *Shukhobor* sets incorporated theme-appropriate dramas that applied biblical principles to everyday situations. Day-to-day scenarios drew the listener in; contextualized dramas strengthened the theme and made the materials culturally appropriate. Bridge narration guided the listener through the audio products. The Bible passages were read several times on each side of the tape for the new reader to read along. The audio products started and ended with Scriptures-in-song. A signature song allowed the listener to identify the *Shukhobor* audio products. Later in the tape, the listener could learn the songs and sing along—so the stories were re-emphasized to the listener. Difficult words were carefully pronounced and explained. The narrators encouraged listeners to attempt the written exercises in the primers.

The audio products were produced in Shanti Bani and Bani Dipti studios. Talented readers with clear diction, professional singers, and musicians were used. Not all of them were Christians.

TABLE 7: FORMAT PLAN FOR *SHUKHOBOR* 3 PRODUCT 1, SIDE A

1.	Signature song
2.	Dialogue between Nagen and Ravi
3.	Drama based on Genesis 12:1-9 (Covenant for blessing and a call for obedience)
4.	Dialogue as a link that introduces the Bible reading text
5.	Bible reading—Genesis 12:1-9
6.	Dialogue—exercises (based on 12: 1-9) announced
7.	Song based on Genesis 12: 1-9
8.	Dialogue—answers to the exercises announced
9.	Signature song

Table 8 is a sample of fictional profiling done on the characters on the tape. The names of the characters are common in rural Bangladesh. Nagen and Ravi interact as student and teacher in the *Shukhobor* series. The student, Nagen, is a seeker of truth and is interested in literacy. He is thirty-five years of age, married, and has children. He is a Hindu (non-fundamental), a new reader, a day-laborer farmer earning a minimum wage and trying to meet his basic needs. His friend is teacher Ravi. The two characters live in the same village, are married, and have children. Yet, they have differences: Ravi, a committed Christian, is a Bible teacher and story-teller. He is ten years older than Nagen, with three more years of formal education. Ravi farms his own land to meet his basic needs, and also has his own radio. He can read newspapers and the Bible.

TABLE 8: CHARACTERIZATION OF NAGEN AND RAVI

	Nagen	**Ravi**
Role	Seeker	Bible teacher,
Age	35	45
Religion	Hindu, but not greatly attached to religious life. He considers all religions to be the same. He likes religious songs.	A committed church going Christian. Likes to read the Bible and tell Bible stories to anyone who wants to listen.
Occupa-tion	Farmer. He does not have any land but works in Khitish Babu's land as a contract worker (Borgachashi). He gets fifty percent of the harvest. He also has time to work as a daily labourer in the lands of Paresh Babu and Madan Babu.	Farmer. He owns one acre of land. He also works as a daily labourer in the lands of Paresh Babu and Madan Babu. He is a good friend of Nagen, who likes to listen to all the good stories from the Bible which Ravi tells.
Income	1000 *taka* per month	1800 *taka* per month

Education	Functionally non-literate. Has studied only up to class 2.	Literate. Has studied up to class 5. Recently attended the adult literacy program in his village. Uses the literacy material of BBS.
Family	Married. Wife, Moina, (27) does not work. Son, Jadu, (10) class 2. Daughter, Rina, (7) not in school. Daughter, Bina, (5) not in school.	Married. Wife, Beauty, (38) sewing work. Daughter, Mary, (15) class 8. Son, David, (10) class 3.
Needs and problems	Money for food, clothes. Lives in a one-room mud house with leaking roof and no proper sanitation. Looking for a bigger house. Sick children have little medical care. Wants his son to discontinue studies in order to join him as a farmer.	Basic necessities are not his problem. Needs a loan to buy more land. Lives in a two-room house with independent kitchen. For medical care, he takes his children to mission hospital. Wants his children to continue studies.

Interests	No radio, TV, newspaper, or Bible in his house. He likes to go to Ravi's house to listen to radio songs/news and Ravi's stories.	Has an AM/FM radio but no TV. Reads newspaper in the teashop. Reads his Bible daily.

Use of Music

Local music gives a familiar flavor to the audio products; popular tunes were used to an advantage of familiarity. In one instance, a Scripture-in-song used a catchy tune about education that was being played regularly on television and radio. People recognized some of the well-known local singers and musicians. Singing the Scriptures reinforced the impact of the Scriptures selected, making them easier to memorize. Music was used as a bridge and local instrumental pieces were dubbed in. Music is entertaining and relaxing, and made learning more fun for the new readers.

Literacy Primer

Primer booklets accompanied the audio products. They included Bible stories and written exercises. Local artists illustrated Bangladeshi life, along with scanned clipart of biblical stories from the UBS-Asia Pacific office.

Making Prototypes

Prototypes of the literacy materials for pre-testing purposes used a cut-and-paste method for the primer and a thirty-minute cassette tape of a reasonably clear recording. These prototypes were pre-tested with the target audience. After participants listened to the tape and tried the primer exercises, they provided important feedback. Several pre-test editions were completed before the products were ready for field testing.

CHAPTER 11

Literacy Materials and Extended Testing

The first set of *Shukhobor* literacy material included an audio product, a primer, two NRP booklets, and a plastic bag to hold the contents. These were tested with thirty groups, evenly divided between men's groups and women's groups. The covers, stickers, bags, and books were color-coded: red for the first set, green for the second, purple for the third, and yellow for the color for the fourth, as illustrated in Table 9. This was to ensure that the materials would not get mixed up.

TABLE 9: COLOR CODING SCHEME FOR THE ENTIRE LITERACY PRODUCTS

	Covers	Stickers	Plastic Bag	Book
SB set 1 vol. 1	Red	Red	Red	Red
SB set 1 vol. 2	Green	Green	Green	Green
SB set 1 vol. 3	Violet	Violet	Violet	Violet
SB set 1 vol. 4	Yellow	Yellow	Yellow	Yellow

Titles and numbers were clearly written on the cover and on the stickers of the audio products. Plastic bags, with the same picture and color as the covers kept the product and primer together. Supplemental New Readers' Portions booklets were also included for extra reading. The end result was presentable to be marketed and sold.

Issues in Group Use

Group dynamics are an important factor in this literacy program. In Bangladesh, separate gender groups generally work well. Men may make the women feel inferior or may not give them a chance to speak in a mixed group. Women feel inhibited when they are with men, but freer to voice their own opinions to other women. Class time is also social time when women escape from the mundane. Meanwhile, the men have an opportunity to learn and improve themselves. In separate gender groups they feel free to discuss matters, without the embarrassment of a woman potentially doing better than they in the class.

Age is a factor in a group; a wide age range has a definite disadvantage because of the differences of shared experiences and maturity. Due to cultural norms of respect, older ones in the group may dominate the conversation while younger ones remain silent.

The group size varied between five and fifteen participants during the test period. However, once extensive testing began, a group of ten was recommended. Compatible levels of literacy within the group were maintained with an entrance evaluation that gauged an individual's literacy skill level.

An egalitarian system of social interaction was encouraged so that all members—regardless of economic conditions and religious beliefs—were treated equally. There should be mutual respect for each other and others' opinions.

Physical conditions conducive for learning included ample lighting by oil lamps and space for a regular meeting place. That was sometimes they met outdoors, sitting on mats or even met in a barn. Blackboards, erasers, chalk, pens, and notebooks were sometimes also supplied to the groups.

Learning in a group meant sharing time and space. Some of the expenses were also shared (for example, money for battery charges). Also, people in the same village share similar problems can discuss and find solutions collectively. To illustrate this, a story is told about a young man being taught about unity by his grandfather. The grandfather told him to gather many sticks and to tie them in a bunch. Try as he might the younger man was not able to break the bundle of sticks. There is strength in unity in a group of people; the spirit of those in the group will not be easily broken. This could applied to village challenges.

In learning together, the group got to know each other well. A sense of trust was built and some groups were able to form a savings group. With combined money there was more possibility to invest, borrow. and lend wisely to make common profits. Self-help was the best help and a community found resources within themselves.

A reading circle is formed when a group will read the same book together and then have a discussion. Each member of the group can take turns in reading a length of passage suitable for each individual. Group members encouraged each other to go on reading. There were songs to be sung together. The group became a choir in harmony with each other.

Issues in Individual Use

Individuals can use these self-contained materials. Some do not have time to join a literacy group. Some prefer to learn on their own for reasons of privacy. Others learn better when they study on their own.

If a person is in a busy or noisy place, it is challenging to learn from the audio products and primers. It is difficult to hear the cassette and focus on the written exercises in the primer. A suitable place and time is needed. Children can be a distraction during study time. It is best to let active children go out to play or to study when they are asleep. With a suitable place and time, it is important to listen carefully to the cassette. Instructions tell when to turn to the pages. Reading along improves reading skills. When the combined letter words are spelled and said, students say them aloud with the guides on the tape.

The workbooks should be done daily. When an exercise is not done daily, the ability to do it well may lessen. This is so with the literacy skills of reading, writing, and counting.

Table 10 summarizes the issues in the use of the materials by groups and individuals.

TABLE 10: SUMMARY OF INDIVIDUAL AND GROUP USE

Use by an individual	Use by a group
S/he needs basic reading skills. S/he needs access to a working cassette player. S/he needs a pen or pencil to write with and an eraser to correct mistakes. S/he needs a place and time for study. S/he needs discipline and motivation to learn. S/he needs to listen to the cassette carefully, doing the lesson on the appropriate side. S/he does the written exercises day-by-day. S/he talks to other people about what has been learnt. S/he practices writing apart from the lesson exercises. S/he reads material other than the primer and the extra reading material. If s/he does not understand something, s/he asks someone who can read and write to explain it. At the end of each set, s/he is tested and upon passing, is given a certificate and prize of a Bible product.	A leader will organize and facilitate the group. The Bible Society trains this facilitator. A group has a common cassette player, battery, and any other materials. Each member should understand the purpose and rules of meeting, as well as upkeep and usage of audio devices. A group meets regularly each week. A group discusses and learns together to help each other. A group can be a reading circle to read and study other materials together. A group can be encouraged to be a savings cooperative to have an economic purpose. At the end of each set, a Field Coordinator assesses the group. Those who pass are given certificates and prizes.

Oversight and Feedback of Literacy Groups

Any successful program must include oversight and supervision. Facilitation, group feedback, and reports help ascertain the success of a literacy campaign as well pointing out needed improvements and adjustments.

Facilitators for Literacy Groups

Men and women from different districts and villages were selected by BLM-D and BLC to facilitate these literacy groups. They were brought together for five days of training. The topics covered:

- Introduction to the need of literacy
- Purpose of the materials
- Benefit of the materials
- Profile of a new reader
- How to treat members of the literacy group
- Responsibilities of a facilitator
- How to use the materials
- Trouble-shooting any difficulties with the audio devices and batteries
- Follow-up of each of the participants

The facilitators were farmers, lay-pastors, and students with at least a grade ten level of education. They were given travel and daily allowances, with an honorarium of five dollars after three months of work. They signed agreements to be responsible for the materials. If any cassette player or battery was spoilt by neglect or sold by design, they had to pay for a replacement. As facilitators recruited group members, they were to clearly articulate that these were Bible-based materials. Those who joined did so of their own freewill. A follow-up workshop was scheduled three months later. Table 11 lists the responsibilities of facilitators.

TABLE 11: FACILITATORS' RESPONSIBILITIES

1.	Guide to and motivate members in the literacy group.
2.	Be accountable to the Field Coordinator or Field Supervisor.
3.	Organize the group to meet regularly.
4.	Keep attendance records.
5.	Explain and demonstrate the use of the materials.
6.	Supply materials such as primers to each group member.
7.	Keep the cassette player and battery clean and functioning.
8.	Inform the Field Coordinator or Field Supervisor of technical problems.
9.	Conduct reading and comprehension assessments for each member and keep a record of results.
10.	Attend all Facilitators' Seminars for training.

Supervision

In order for extensive testing to be conducted well, there was a need for supervision. The BLM-D employed a Field Coordinator with this job description:

- Oversee and coordinate reading circles in particular areas or districts determined by the church.
- Work in cooperation with pastors and church committees, keeping them informed and involved in the program.
- Participate in the selection and hiring process of circle facilitators.
- Continuously tabulate and update circle members' biographical information plus monitor reading and comprehension progress.
- Teach the facilitators how to use the cassette and text system and to emphasize to them their responsibilities of

attendance, record keeping, and the help that they can give as a guide.
- Motivate the facilitators by encouraging them and praying with them.
- Pay out any remuneration or stipends to the facilitators, keeping proper receipts.
- Have a working and technical knowledge of audio products and batteries, in particular and how to maintain them in good working order and how to detect what is wrong with them.
- Supply the necessary equipment, audio devices, and batteries and to distribute the necessary materials, audio products, primers, notebooks, pens, supplementary audio products, and reading material.
- Keep contracts or agreements on the audio devices so that if they are damaged or resold the facilitators are held responsible.
- Plan and schedule circle visits, which must be handed in to the supervising authorities.
- Periodically visit each reading circle to check on students' progress.
- Submit proper accounts on cash advances for facilitators' stipends, purchases, seminar expenditure and official travel expenses.
- Write progress reports for the supervising authorities.

When the geographical area became too widespread to be supervised by one person, a second level of Field Supervisors was engaged to help the Field Coordinator. They were not full-time workers but had the same responsibilities as the Field Coordinator, only with a limited number of groups in their immediate area. They had the most contact with the facilitators.

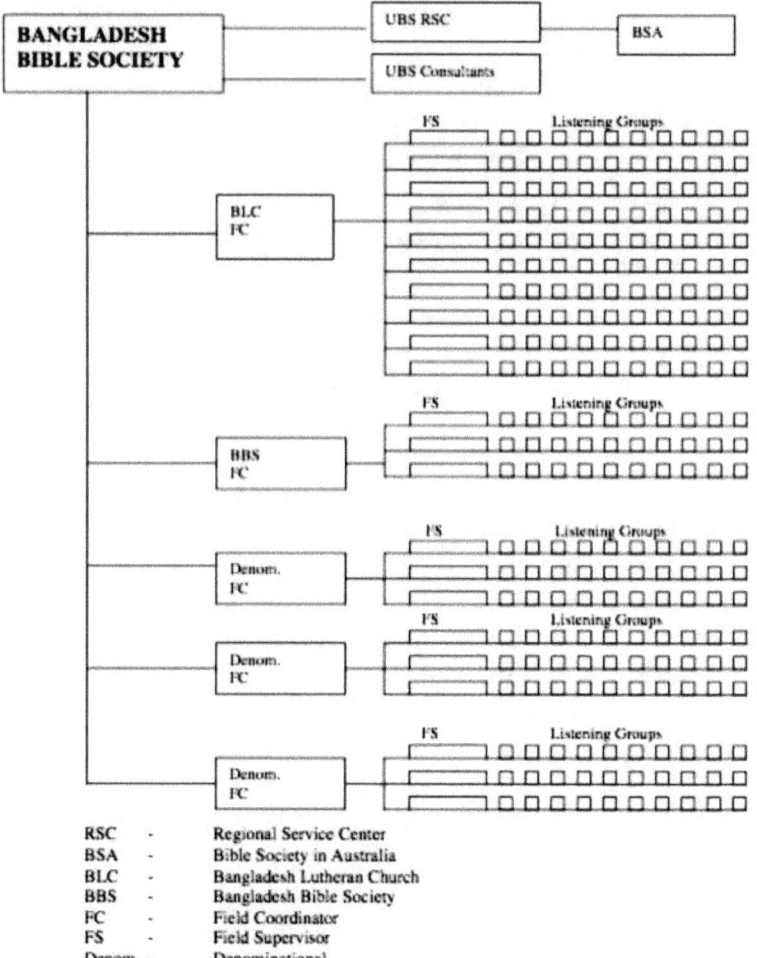

FIGURE 6 PROGRAM MANAGEMENT SYSTEM
(Søgaard 1998 Report for UBS)

Program Management System

Figure 6 illustrates the program management system used for accountability, quality control, and supervision. The BBS, as the local Bible Society, was the channel for coordinating this program. Providing advice and sending the necessary technical support of Media and Translation Consultants was the UBS regional office for the Asia-Pacific Region Bible societies. The Bible Society of Australia provided funding for the later development of the program for literacy groups formed for other denominations.

The actual outworking of the program was in the listening groups. These groups consisted of ten participants, and there were ten groups under the supervision of one Field Supervisor. These Field Supervisors were answerable to the Field Coordinator. The original literacy groups were formed by BLC. These were followed by groups formed by Bangladesh Bible Society with their own Field Coordinator and Supervisors. The most recent developments showed other denominations were using these materials with their own Field Coordinators and Supervisors.

Follow-up and Regular Monitoring

The Field Coordinator conducted follow-up visits with each facilitator, so he was constantly on the move. Every three months, there were two-day follow-up sessions where facilitators could present their reports. They were given their honorarium and the next set of materials. Feedback from the groups played an important role in improving the materials. It was also important to track the learner progress with attendance records, reading and comprehension tests, and give progress rewards to maintain learner interests and motivation.

CHAPTER 12

Distribution and Testimonials

Using audio products for an adult literacy program was a new concept. A list was compiled of possible persons, groups, and organizations that would use these adult literacy materials. They were introduced to these new materials and how they could be used. Mainly, denominational and Christian mission leaders were interested.

It is not possible for everyone to own a cassette player and audio products. However, an organization, a group, or an even individual could borrow these materials. For this program to run in an effective way, a cassette loan system was set up. A record was kept of the distribution and use of each cassette. The BLC synod committee was appointed to have oversight of the program.

A membership fee that was affordable by most villagers was required. This amount was used for battery charging and other expenses. This small fee also gave each member of the literacy group ownership of the program, committing them to attend regularly since they were paying for it.

Listening Devices

Commercial devices were cheaper and easier to repair. Some of the village people have never used such a device before and needed to be taught how to use it. The device was kept covered in a plastic bag or wrapped with a cloth to keep it as dust free as possible. It was to be kept in a safe place so that it would not be stolen or damaged. Major repairs were not to be attempted; it was to be sent to a repair shop in town.

Batteries: Types, Use, and Care

The literacy groups used rechargeable batteries. Unfortunately, they did not always use the best batteries as these did not last long and had to be replaced within a year. The facilitators were instructed that the batteries should be kept in a dry place.

A new battery could run a device for many hours. When the charge was used up, the new charge might run for a shorter period of time.

Potential Difficulties

The facilitators were instructed on how to handle potential difficulties that affected the wear and tear of the device and batteries. For example, if the audio product was no longer playing, they should contact the coordinator for a replacement. Other problems might be something wrong with the device itself or the battery. The equipment should be checked carefully by facilitators.

Budgetary Considerations

Finances were provided through a literacy fund from the Danish Mission and Bible Society of Australia. Major expense items were budgeted during the various stages of the project.

TABLE 12: BUDGET ITEMS PER TEST PERIOD

Test Period	
1.	Salary for research assistant to develop and test the materials
2.	Operations: travel, room and board
3.	Expenses for pre-testing and monitoring
4.	Prototype: photocopies, studio work, and printing
5.	Reporting: translation in Bengali for BBS Board, faxes, telephone calls, and postage
Extensive testing and initial production	
1.	Studio rental and technicians
2.	Payment to artists, songwriters, and translators
3.	Duplication of audio products

4.	Computer formatting, especially in Bengali word-processing
5.	Printing primers
6.	Salaries of coordinators, supervisors, and facilitators
7.	Operations: including travel, room and board
8.	Evaluation: copies of survey forms and payment to interviewers
Full production	
1.	Studio rental and technicians
2.	Printing primers
3.	Miscellaneous expenses
4.	Monitoring and evaluation: including copies of survey forms and payment to interviewers

During the early testing period, the UBS in the Asia Pacific Region funded a research assistant's salary for approximately two and half years. Funding also included operational expenses for travel, translators, and communication with UBS consultants. Several pre-tests entailed production of audio products and primers, as well as evaluative feedback from the target audience. A larger scale pre-test was conducted with prototype sets for *Shukhobor* Set 1 and *Muktir Path* Set 1, including eight master audio products plus ten copies of each tape, one hundred primers, and booklet on the *Life of Christ*. The UBS fund was also used for the report at the end of the test period.

When the product was ready for extensive testing, the Danish Missionary Council Development Office funded it as a mini-project that would benefit the BLC. This fund covered the development of both tracks of the literacy materials, audio devices, batteries, and audio products for 160 groups. It paid for recharging batteries, maintaining audio devices, training seminars, and travel by the Field Coordinator. Salaries for the Field Coordinators and Supervisors were paid by the Danish Mission. Each member of the literacy groups paid two *taka* a week for their pens and notebooks.

Finally, the Bible Society of Australia provided the Bangladesh Bible Society with literacy grant funds to produce the materials for distribution. In this stage, there were studio expenses for re-taping the parts of the audio that needed editing. The primers and reading booklets were printed in bulk. Some miscellaneous expenses were not categorized.

Testimonials

Most of these problems were overcome. BBS saw many positive results. First, non-literates who participated were becoming functionally literate. Within a year of participation, non-literates could read aloud the stories. Second, a community spirit was cultivated between Christian, Hindu, and Muslim group members. In the past, villagers would not associate with each other; through these literacy groups they came together. They pooled their financial resources in a savings cooperative. Hindus and Muslims showed goodwill towards Christians. They genuinely liked the good stories and they asked the Christians questions about Jesus. Third, women were allowed to study. Even in the mixed-gender groups, women voiced their own opinions. The following are four testimonies from Christian women in the more recent literacy groups under the supervision of the BBS.

Martha and Ananda

Jotsna Barikder is a literacy group facilitator in the Bangladesh Baptist Church at Kaligram in Gopalgonj district. Her brother Ananda and his wife Martha were both non-literate. Jotsna is younger than her brother and felt embarrassed to teach him. So she planned to help him by including Martha in her literacy group.

Martha spent more than a year-and-a-half in a literacy class and learned to read and write. Before joining the group, she did not even know the Bengali alphabet. As Jotsna helped develop her sister-in-law's reading skills, Martha could teach her husband and also help her children with their school homework.

After their evening meal, Martha usually sat with Ananda and helped him write the alphabet. When she faced any difficulties with teaching, she went to her sister-in-law and asked for her help. In the beginning, Ananda felt embarrassed to learn from his wife but he was encouraged by his wife who helped him understand the benefits of literacy for his life. Slowly he began to recognize the alphabet and was writing his name. Now he refuses to use finger printing and instead he prefers to sign for any payments, even though his handwriting is not that good.

Ananda understood that by learning to read and write, he could better himself. He continued learning from his wife, Martha, and she was determined to teach him enough so that he would be able to read the Bible by himself (Joydhor 1999:1-2).

Shova

Shova Bairagee returned to her own village with her husband and children from the city, Khulna, a few years ago. Since she could not find any jobs she decided to open a snack shop in her village where the villagers could come and eat. Her husband helped her to run this shop.

Shova, age twenty-five, one of the members of the Kaligram literacy group, was working hard to support her family as well as trying to learn to read and write. Anil Bairagee, her husband, age thirty-six, always encouraged her to attend the literacy class. He realized the benefits of attending the class. He said to her, "We are fools because we did not attend school, but we will encourage our children to attend school, and we will guide them so that they may develop their skills."

Shova had been learning with the group for more than a year. She feels that she is wiser and is getting many blessings from the Lord. She has a happy family and some of the literacy group members were her customers, too. They were glad to buy snacks from their fellow group member, Shova (Joydhor 1999:3-4).

Shobita

Soon after Shobita Mazumder was married she joined in a literacy class conducted in the Bangladesh Baptist Fellowship Church in Gopalgonj. She did not read the Bible regularly, but later she read her Bible daily. She learned many things that helped her to help her family.

Shobita had formal schooling for nine years. She also encouraged her mother-in-law to listen to the audio products. She felt that through this program even the non-literates can benefit because they can listen and share with others.

Shobita's husband was an electrical technician and he worked in the town. He encouraged her to attend the class regularly. There were ten to twelve members in this literacy group (Joydhor 1999:5-6).

Lata

Lata Baroi, age thirty-two, married when she was thirteen years old. She joined the literacy class when it started in their area. She studied in formal schooling for five years, but after she got married she stopped her studies and for the eighteen years she was busy with her family.

She said, "Now I have the courage to talk with people and I encourage others to attend the literacy group. I heard the stories from the birth of Jesus up to His resurrection. Before this class I did not know these stories in detail."

After being in the class, Lata could read for herself. She had three sons and two daughters. Her elder son studied in Barisal Baptist Mission School in Class 9. Her husband, a fisherman, encouraged her to learn to read and write. Lata said, "I had a little knowledge from school but I learned a lot from this literacy group. It has helped me in reading, writing and has also helped me in my spiritual life" (Joydhor 1999:7-8).

Summary

This experimental literacy project in Bangladesh was made possible through partnerships. There were multiple partnerships among UBS, BBS, BLM-D, BLC, other churches, along with the support from the Bible Society of Australia and Danish Mission organizations. People in the villages were gracious enough to participate in the testing of these materials and give honest feedback.

Two tracks of literacy materials developed in Bangladesh use primers and audio products. The first track, *Shukhobor* or Good News, was created for new readers in the villages. These materials grade gradually from beginner to intermediate to functional literacy.

Themes are based on the needs of the people and use appropriate Bible stories to address these needs. The second track, called *Muktir Path* or Path of Salvation, was developed for Christian new readers and gives a broad survey of the Bible, including the life of Christ, Old Testament characters, New Testament epistles, and major Christian topics such as faith, giving, and salvation.

Challenges in the Bengali language include the complex combine-letter words and different types of Bengali. The development of the materials was a team effort by people with differing talents and expertise in theology, literacy, and media. In script-writing and primer-writing workshops after the test period, some wrote the scripts and primers. Music, illustrations, and any other inclusions into the materials were done within the context of Bangladesh. However, it can be done in other countries as well.

The series were produced after rigorous testing. Materials were color-coded to distinguish each set of cassette and primer. An elaborate management system was developed for accountability, supervision, and feedback. It involved an inverted pyramid of the people in the villages to those in executive positions. On the field, there were coordinators, supervisors, and facilitators.

An individual can use these self-contained materials. Groups can also effectively use them because they employ group dynamics in the pedagogy. Practical information explained how to use and take care of audio devices and batteries, as well as how to solve potential difficulties. Budgetary considerations included major expense items in three phases of pre-testing, extensive testing, and full production. Shared investment from different organizations was added to contributions from the participants. Four testimonies from women in the program illustrate how this literacy program has impacted their lives in a real and positive way.

Development of theory and experimentation has resulted in experience as well as derivation of communication, contextual, and conceptual principles. If the concepts of these materials are to be taken to other countries, they should be adapted. Translating these materials may not be helpful because they were created for Bangladesh. Each country and culture is unique. Therefore, local music, dramas, artwork, as well as language must be used appropriately. Partnership with national churches and denominations would also be important. Systems for distribution, monitoring, and evaluation should be worked out depending on each situation.

CHAPTER 13

Timeline of the Literacy Project

PROJECT Research activities related to this program began in October 1990 with a baseline research study of the literacy situation in northern Bangladesh. Field tests were conducted between 1991 and 1999. The main study on the specific literacy program managed by the BLM-D was conducted in villages where there was a BLC congregation. It used Scripture-focused and media-based literacy materials produced by the BBS.

Early Research

Research was done in two parts. The first happened from 1990 to 1999. The second part was field research in 2000.

Brief Summary of Baseline Research Conducted in 1990

First, I used a random sample of one hundred past students of whom forty-four percent were Hindus, thirty-seven percent Muslim, and nineteen percent were Christian. These former students were from classes conducted from 1987 to 1989, with sixty-two percent from 1988 to 1989 (Chai 1990:29). Second, a reading and comprehension evaluation was given on two categories of reading material. The first category was a passage from the primer they had studied in their literacy program, so they were familiar with the passage. The second category was from the first booklet of the NRP, a simplified text of the wise and foolish builders in Matthew 7:24-27. With one comprehension question for each of these passages, forty-nine percent could read the primer passage with comprehension. In the second category of reading the NRP, only ten percent could read the Scriptural passage with comprehension. Third, they were surveyed for their opinions on learning literacy, especially the area of motivation (Chai 1990:45-47).

This baseline survey showed that the largest age group of respondents were twenty to twenty-nine, more than half were married, with an almost equal numbers of men and women respondents in the sample. Most worked as farmers. Seventy percent had a high perceived value of literacy (Chai 1990:73-74).

Many factors affected the learners' motivation:

- high physical energy level
- improvement of social status
- encouragement by family and friends
- practical content of the curriculum
- good literacy teachers
- length and frequency of their course was doable
- follow-up given by supervisors of the program
  The respondents were also enthusiastic about the inclusion of audio products with good stories (Chai 1990:75-76).

Testing and Production Development from 1991-1994

October 1991 to July 1994 was a period of product development with field testing. The actual research consisted of three phases:

- Phase I was baseline research (see previous section).
- Phase II was product development and testing (reported in this section).
- Phase III covered the extensive use of completed materials and their long-term effects and the publication of a full report and necessary material (Søgaard 1991:1).
  There are two components in Phase II:
- development of a multi-media approach to literacy training, primarily using print and audio products.
- integration of Scripture into a literacy program.

Also, there were three guidelines for the testing of the audio products:

- Did it provide motivation to read?
- Did it effectively communicate the Scriptures?
- Did it improve reading skills including understanding?

Phase II tested the use of audio products with the printed text to see if this combination could improve reading and the comprehension skills of the user. The audio product used dramatic presentations, as well as various other art forms, such as music and songs, to communicate the Scriptures effectively. The primers contained the Bible stories, written exercises, word explanations, and pictures.

The village-based literacy materials of *Shukhobor* Set 1 or "Good News for a Friend" went through many test versions before the first set was completed. The first field test lasted three weeks. Variables of age, gender, whether a savings group component were used, whether a group was Christian-only or a mix of religions, and individual versus group use. There were approximately fifty participants in this field test. The age range was between twelve and forty, eighty-five percent were male, with a nearly a fifty-fifty mix of marrieds and singles. Fifty-nine percent were Hindus, twenty-eight percent were Christians, and thirteen percent were Muslims (Chai 1990:2).

Table 13 summarizes the reading and comprehension after the three weeks of testing. Unlike the earlier reading and comprehension evaluation of 1990, this was an elaborate evaluation with five reading material categories that ranged from easy to difficult. However, the evaluative standard for reading and comprehension remained the same. It is interesting to note that a person may be able to read but not necessarily with comprehension, which explains the difference in the two columns.

TABLE 13: SUMMARY OF READING AND COMPREHENSION RESULTS

Reading Category	Reading Results		Comprehension Results	
Primer text from former literacy curriculum	Read well	44%	Correct answer	27%
	Read quite well	22%	Partially correct answer	22%
	Read haltingly	22%	Wrong answer	40%
	Could not read at all	12%	No answer	12%
A Bible story from *Shukhobor*	Read well	27%	Correct answer	27%
	Read quite well	31%	Partially correct answer	11%
	Read haltingly	25%	Wrong answer	25%
	Could not read at all	17%	No answer	37%
New readers' newspaper	Read well	22%	Correct answer	14%
	Read quite well	17%	Partially correct answer	17%
	Read haltingly	29%	Wrong answer	20%
	Could not read at all	32%	No answer	49%
Wise and Foolish Builder from Common Language New Testament	Read well	29%	Correct answer	37%
	Read quite well	27%	Partially correct answer	17%
	Read haltingly	20%	Wrong answer	7%
	Could not read at all	24%	No answer	39%
Regular newspaper	Read well	22%	Correct answer	51%
	Read quite well	27%	Partially correct answer	15%
	Read haltingly	19%	Wrong answer	10%
	Could not read at all	32%	No answer	24%

Participants of the field test responded that the audio products were understandable, helpful in the reading of the stories, made the teaching of the combined-letter words easier, and that the Scriptures-in-song helped them learn the songs and remember the lessons. The pictures in the primers illustrated the stories well. Volunteer facilitators thought that the level of the materials was no higher than grade four and that not too many words were used. They all agreed that the materials helped the reading abilities of participants. Church leaders who evaluated these audio products said the chosen Bible stories were appropriate to the needs of the people. They like the songs which they thought had meaningful words and could encourage, teach, influence thinking, and entertain.

Between 1992 and 1993, a longer field test was conducted with eighteen groups. The testing started with 132 participants, ended with 127, and lasted for two months. Initial and post reading results were done. There was a ten to fifteen percent increase in reading and comprehension skills within the test period in the reading category of "The Wise and Foolish Builder." There was an eighteen percent difference from the baseline results of 1990. Compared to the three-week field test, the results were nearly the same in that category, but there was an increase of fifteen to twenty percent in the reading and comprehension in primer, Bible story, and newspaper categories (see Table 13).

Two field tests were done for the development of *Muktir Path* Set 1. The first one was conducted with sixty-six respondents and the second with 103, all members of BLC. Most participants listened to the audio products more than two times. In a survey, the sixty-six respondents indicated that the Scripture readings and songs were clear and they were able to sing along. Certain words in the story were explained which made them more understandable. They liked the voices used; the speed of reading seemed natural. The dialogue on the audio products was easy to follow: they heard the announcement of the page numbers, could find the page, and read along with the audio products. Almost all were willing to either buy or borrow these audio products and, if they played them in their homes, more than ten persons would be able to listen to them. About twenty-five percent were new readers in these samples.

The feedback from these field tests was positive. The changes from the prototype to the ready product were improved sound clarity of the audio, printing and not photocopying the primers, and color covers for cassette jackets, primer covers, and matching plastic bags for packaging. These materials in the more completed and polished form was ready for more extensive monitoring.

Monitoring of Program from 1995-1997

Between July 1995 and June 1997, the BBS and the BLC were given a grant from the Danish Missionary Council Development Office (DMCDO). This grant was used to complete the production of masters for the remaining two sets of *Shukhobor*, the remaining three sets of *Muktir Path*, as well as the implementation of the whole literacy program with BLM-D and BLC literacy groups in villages, over a period of two years.

In August 1995, the first thirty of 160 total groups were initiated in the district of Nilphamari, Bangladesh. A total of 160 groups was proposed as these would cover eighty different BLC locations and comply with the ideal of separate gender groups. The groups started over the course of 1995 and 1996: Nilphamari August in 1995, Pirganj in October 1995, Birganj and Kaharol in March and April 1996, and Naogaon in May 1996. Approximately 1,600 were participating by the time it was fully operational in 1996 (Chai 1995:1).

By August 1996, there were fifteen men's groups and fifteen women's groups in Pirganj, which contained 205 Christians, 95 Hindus, and no Muslims. There were 126 women and 174 men for a total of 300 persons. In Nilphamari there were only twelve women's groups and eighteen men's groups. Of the 300 people, 179 were Christian, 113 were Hindu, and four were Muslim. There were 119 women and 187 men, giving a total of 296. The total from the two areas was 596. An analysis of the attendance records of these groups in June showed that the average attendance was about ninety-three percent, no group had 100 percent attendance, but no group's attendance was below eighty percent either (Chai 1996:2).

At the end of this two-year period, an evaluation was conducted randomly among twenty groups from the five districts, composed of approximately 200 respondents. The evaluation showed an improvement in the reading and comprehension of participants. Respondents were asked for feedback about the audio products and primers: they indicated that the sound quality of the audio products was clear and the primers were easy to use. The audio products helped them in their reading. They had listened to the same audio product at least six times in a week. They most liked the stories and songs on the audio products. More than half of the respondents found reading the primers easy and the size of the font suitable. However, the written exercises were challenging. They liked the pictures in the primers. Christian respondents indicated that their understanding of the passages was increased.

Field Research in April 2000

BLC literacy groups started in 1996. BBS started other literacy groups in partnership with local churches in November 1997, once the literacy program was fully functional with complete sets of materials. BBS employed three supervisors to oversee the new groups formed in Mymensingh, Gopalganj, Rajshahi, and Bogra.

April 5-9, 2000, surveys were conducted in six different districts: Mymensingh, Gopalganj, Rajshahi, Bogra, Dinajpur and Nilphamari. 299 members of the literacy groups were surveyed. Local volunteers conducted the survey using a standard questionnaire with individual respondents.

The survey studied the effects of the media-based and Scripture-focused literacy program in Bangladesh (see Table 14).

TABLE 14: RESEARCH OBJECTIVES

Objective: Description
Information goals
Objective 1: To obtain demographic information on the users during 1996 to 1999
Age of respondent
Gender of respondent
Marital status of respondent
Occupation of respondent
Economic status of respondent
Religion of respondent
Ethnicity of respondent
Geographical location of respondent
Previous education of respondent
Length of time respondent has been in the program

Objective 2: To study the cognitive, affective, and behavioral effects on sociocultural and religious attitudes caused by the literacy program
Are there any effects of knowledge, attitude, and behavior on learning to read?
Are there any effects of knowledge, attitude, and behavior towards the Bible?
Are there any effects of knowledge, attitude, and behavior towards Christianity?
Is there a difference in these effects for Hindus and Muslims?
What is the influence of group dynamics?
Objective 3: To study the literacy effects on the participants
What are the effects on the reading abilities of the respondents?
What are the effects on the comprehension abilities of the respondents?
What are the effects on the writing abilities of the respondents?
What are the effects on the abilities to do simple accounting for daily use?
Compare effects on new reader users.
Objective 4: To analyze the distribution use and supervisory system
How should the materials be used?
Comparisons between the uses of the two tracks of materials.
How has the program been supervised?
How should follow-up to the program be done?
Objective 5: To study the impact of the literacy program on the local churches
How many groups were formed under each church?
How many new converts were there as a direct result of the program?
How were the church members affected by the program?
How were church leaders affected by the program?
Has Bible reading increased?
Has Bible knowledge increased?
Has renewed Christian behavior been seen?
The comparisons between the different churches and the Lutheran church as to the effects of the program.

I had five major research objectives. The first objective was to collect demographic information. Data came from those directly involved in this program: new readers, field supervisors, and leaders of the churches hosting the groups. The second objective was to cross-tabulate the demographics with observable sociocultural and religious effects. The third objective was to evaluate the literacy skills of the participants and observations of the supervisors. The fourth objective was to have information on distribution and supervision was received from the supervisors and church leaders who oversaw the program. Finally, the fifth objective was to record the observable impact on the churches, which the church leaders reported. Table 15 shows the correspondence between the objectives of information needs and the sources of information.

TABLE 15: RESEARCH DESIGN

Objective	Participants	Supervisors	Church Leaders
Demographic information	X		
Effects sociocultural and religious attitudes	X	X	X
Literacy effects	X	X	
Distribution and supervision		X	X
Impact on churches			X

Table 16 shows the sources of information and the number of persons in each sample. The participants were randomly selected from groups in each district. The supervisors were the four who had been working in the program. The church leaders were from churches using the materials.[1]

TABLE 16: SAMPLING PLAN

Population	Sample Size	Data Collection Form	Data Tabulation Software
Participants	300	Questionnaires and tests	Abstat
Supervisors	5	Questionnaires	Abstat & MS Excel
Church leaders	10	Questionnaires and interviews	Abstat & MS Excel

---

[1] Refer to Appendixes 2, 3, and 4 for translations of questionnaires used. Appendix 2 is the questionnaire for the new readers, Appendix 3 is the questionnaire for the supervisors, and Appendix 4 is the questionnaire for the church leaders.

As stated above, objective 2 studied the sociocultural and religious effects. Effects in knowledge and skills are quantifiable, whereas attitudinal and behavioral effects are dependent on the responses given by the participants, and not actual observed changes. Objective 3 was the most quantifiable because it used actual reading and comprehension tests. It shows the reading and comprehension levels of the respondents. Objective 4 was mainly a system analysis of distribution and supervision as it was conducted in Bangladesh. This was mainly from the perspective of the supervisors and the coordinator. Objective 5 was to study the impact on local churches. The main church that used the program from the beginning is the BLC. However, from 1998 to 1999, we opened this program for wider distribution and use. Included in this study was a sample of the more recent groups.

CHAPTER 14

Demographics of the Literacy Project

Data was collected from a variety of participants. This section profiles respondents in terms of age, gender, marital status, employment, religion, racial background, economic status and location.

Age

The group between 21 and 30 years of age was forty-five point two percent, twenty-two point four percent were between 31 to 40 years of age, and nineteen point four percent were 15 to 20 years of age. However, only nine point seven percent were above 40 and three point three percent were below 15 years of age.

Gender

The first literacy groups formed under BLC followed the guideline of fifty percent female groups and fifty percent male groups. Under the supervision of the BBS, there were more women in the groups. For this reason, seventy three point six percent of the respondents in this sample were female. The literacy rate among men was forty-nine point four percent, while among women it was only twenty-six point one percent. The program emphasized the need for increasing literacy skills among women.

Marital Status

Eighty point three percent of the respondents were married and fourteen point seven percent were single. Only three point three percent were widowed and one point seven percent did not answer.

Occupation

About fifty-one point three percent of the respondents were housewives. A smaller percentage, five point three percent, were students and three percent were business or working people. Fifteen point four percent owned their own farmland and twenty-four point four percent were day-laborers.

Religious and Racial Groupings

Groups under the BLC were more religiously mixed than those under BBS, with mainly Hindu participants and a few Muslims. Groups under the BBS supervision were composed mainly of Christians; thus, the high percentage of Christians in this sample is as seen in Figure 7.

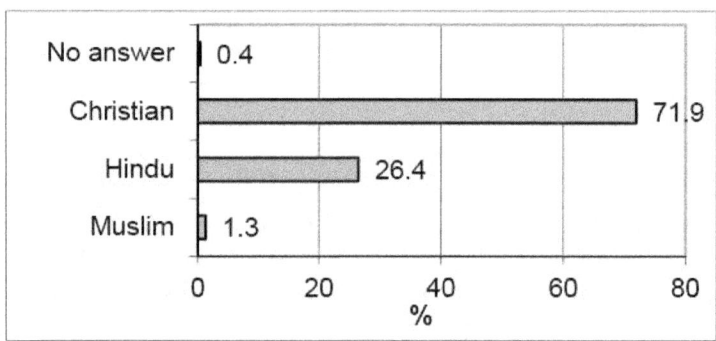

FIGURE 7 RELIGIONS OF THE RESPONDENTS BY PERCENTAGE

Even though the materials are in Bengali, other ethnic groups wanted to learn literacy in the *lingua franca,* or trade language. In fact, since Bengali would be their second language, these learners paid even more attention to the grammar and other technicalities of learning the language. Pahari tribal groups accounted for seven percent of the learners, six percent were Santali, and fourteen point four percent were Garo.

Location

The respondents lived in villages located in six districts. Groups in Rajshahi and Bogra were counted together because these two neighboring districts were under one supervisor. The BBS directly supervised groups in Mymensingh, Rajshahi, Bogra and Gopalganj in partnership with local denominational churches. BLC supervised the groups in Dinajpur and Nilphamari. Respondents from Nilphamari were seventeen point seven percent, twenty-seven point four percent were from Dinajpur, sixteen point seven percent were from Gopalganj, twenty-three point one percent were from Rajshahi and Bogra, and fifteen point one percent were from Mymensingh.

Previous Educational Background

Respondents were asked, "Before joining this group what kind of literacy education did you have?" Figure 8 shows the results of the responses. Some non-literates, twenty-three point one percent, were allowed to join the groups even though these materials were written for new readers. On the other hand, ten point seven percent had reached secondary level education and those in this category were excluded in the report: this group of people would skew the results.

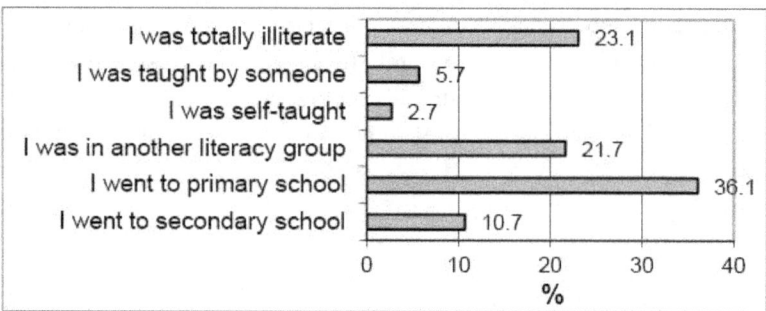

FIGURE 8 EDUCATIONAL LEVELS OF THE RESPONDENTS BY PERCENTAGE

Length of Time in the Literacy Program

Respondents joined the program at different times. In 1999, a total of thirty-eight point 1 percent started the program, with twenty point seven percent starting in mid-year; twenty-seven point four percent began in 1998; thirteen point four percent started in 1997; and point three percent started in 1996.

Summary of Demographic Information

The easiest way to illustrate the demographic information is to make a chart of the information gathered from this survey. Table 17 highlights this information.

Table 17: SUMMARY OF DEMOGRAPHIC INFORMATION

Age of respondents		Location of Respondents	
Below 15 years	3.3%	Nilphamari	17.7%
15-20 years old	19.4%	Dinajpur	27.4%
21-30 years old	45.2%	Gopalganj	16.7%
31-40 years old	22.4%	Rajshahi/Bogra	23.1%
Above 40 years	9.7%	Mymensingh	15.1%
Gender of Respondents		**Educational Background of Respondents**	
Female	73.6%		
Male	26.4%	Non-literate	23.1%
Marital Status of Respondents		Taught by someone	5.7%
Married	80.3%	Self-taught	2.7%
Single	14.7%	Literacy group	21.7%
Widowed	3.3%	Primary school	36.1%
No answer	1.7%	Secondary school	10.7%
Occupation of Respondents		**Length of Time in Program**	
Housewives	51.3%	Mid-1999	20.7%
Students	5.3%	1999	31.8%
Business/work	3.0%	1998	27.4%
Own land	15.4%	1997	13.4%
Day-laborer	24.4%	1996	.3%
Religions of the Respondents		**Ethnic groups**	
Christian	71.9%	Pahari	7%
Hindu	26.4%	Santali	6.7%
Muslim	1.3%	Garo	14.4%
No answer	0.4%		

CHAPTER 15

The Effects of Literacy Project on Sociocultural and Religious Attitudes

Respondents indicated which set of the literacy materials they completed. This information was important in order to determine how much knowledge and exposure the respondents already had through the program. All groups had completed *Shukhobor* Set 1. It is interesting to note that the Hindu and Muslim participants chose to continue with the *Muktir Path* series. At the time of the survey, seventeen point one percent of the respondents were doing *Shukhobor* Set 2, and thirty-three point four percent were doing *Shukhobor* Set 3. Participants doing *Muktir Path* Set 1 were nineteen point seven percent, eight percent had started *Muktir Path* Set 2, another six point four percent were doing *Muktir Path* Set 3, and fifteen point four percent had begun *Muktir Path* Set 4.

Effects of Learning to Read on Knowledge, Attitude, and Behavior

Respondents chose from multiple answers to many of the questions. However, they also expressed some answers in their own words. They were asked, "Why did you want to learn to read?" These results are shown in Figure 9.

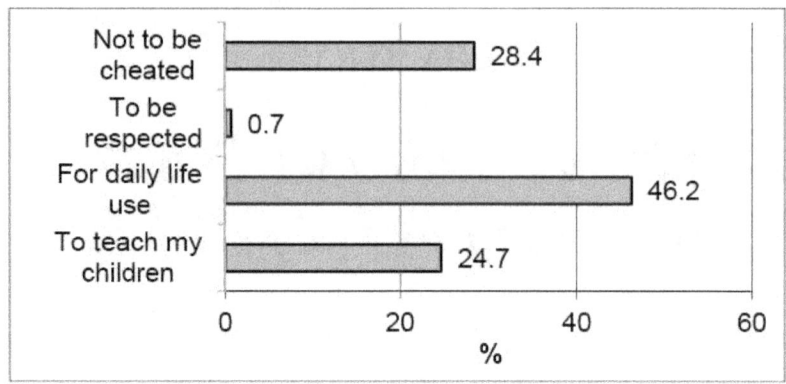

FIGURE 9 REASONS RESPONDENTS WANTED TO LEARN BY PERCENTAGE

Some respondents wrote a sentence to express why they joined the literacy group:
- I don't want to be cheated anymore by others.
- I want to write something.
- I want to give up illiteracy.
- I am now able to write.
- I have learned many things.
- I want to learn more.
- I feel that the stories about Jesus are good.
- I want to know more about Jesus' stories.
- The literacy classes are good for me.
- I want to learn something.
- I want to get more knowledge.
- I want to progress in life.
- I want to teach my children.
- I want some more education and want to know about religious topics.
- I want to learn writing and reading.
- I want to be able to do practical everyday accounting.
- I feel good about the classes.
- I want to learn more of the Bible.

- I want to know more about Bible stories.
- I joined because I love God.
- I get some pleasure from the classes.
- I get much help from these classes.
- I want to learn about Jesus Christ.
- I love the class.
- I come to learn.
- I feel that it is necessary for my life.
- I know that it is necessary for our daily life.
- I joined the classes so that I can improve my Christian life.
- I want to learn well.
- I want to improve my spiritual life.
- I want to grow in my Christian life.
- I joined for my studies.
- I want to teach for others.
- I want to be prosperous.

The written answers fell into the categories listed in Figure 8, with an additional category of "spiritual reasons" ranging from wanting to know more about Christ to growing in their spiritual life.

Effects on Knowledge, Attitude, and Behavior toward the Bible

The questionnaire used the term "good stories" instead of "Bible stories" so as not to offend the non-Christian respondents. However, they knew these were Bible stories as the introduction of the materials clearly communicated this from the beginning. Those that said they had heard some of these stories were forty-seven point five percent, but thirty-three point one percent had never heard them before. Only five point seven had read all the stories, thirteen percent reported that they had read many of the stories, and point seven gave no answer.

When respondents were asked, "What do you think of these stories?" eighty-seven point six percent thought the Bible stories were practical for their lives, eight point seven percent said that the stories were only good for Christians, and another three percent thought that the stories were good for children. Only point seven percent said that the stories were not good for them.

After the completion of the program, sixty-five point six percent indicated that they would read the books again, twenty-seven point seven percent would give them to others to use, and six point seven said they would keep them. None of the respondents chose either to sell or destroy the materials.

Effect on Knowledge, Attitude, and Behavior toward Christianity

Respondents were asked, "What do you know about the Christian religion?" Their answers are listed in Figure 10.

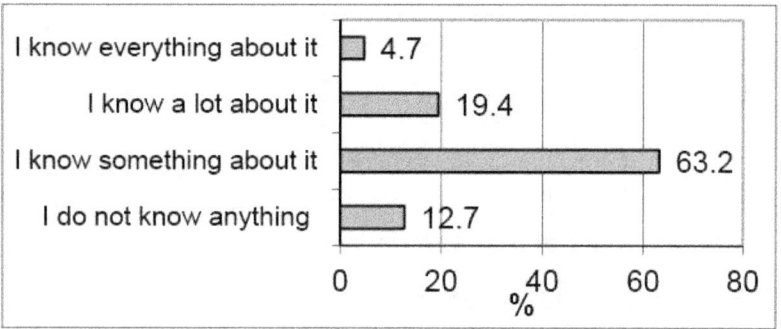

FIGURE 10 RESPONDENTS' KNOWLEDGE ABOUT CHRISTIANITY

When asked, "What do you think about the Christian religion?" ninety-three point three percent said that Christianity was a good religion and five point seven percent were neutral. Only point seven did not like this religion and point three said that it is not a good religion.

The respondents were then asked, "What would you do if you could accept this religion?" The response included sixty-eight point nine percent who said they had already accepted this religion, twenty-one point seven percent indicated that they wanted to know more, three point three percent said that they would accept this religion, and the remaining six point seven percent would not want to accept this religion.

Differences in Effects on Hindus and Muslims

The above results were cross-tabulated based on religion, excluding Christians. The sample contained twenty six point four percent Hindus and one point three percent Muslims. They were asked, "Have you heard these 'good stories' before joining the group?" Their responses are seen in Figure 11.

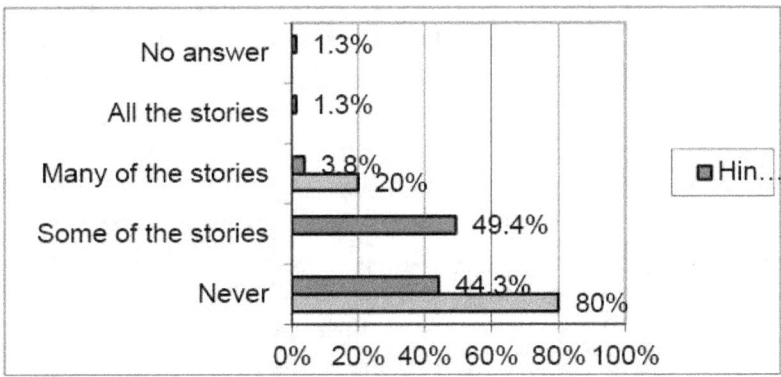

FIGURE 11 KNOWLEDGE OF "GOOD STORIES" BEFORE THE CLASS BEGAN

None of the respondents thought that the stories were too childish. Instead 100 percent of Muslims and seventy-eight point five percent of Hindus thought that these were practical life-application stories. Only two point five percent of Hindus said that these were not good stories for them; the remaining nineteen percent said that these stories were only for Christians. The implication of this response is that there is a high receptivity among the Muslims, and moderately high among the Hindus to practical life application from Bible stories.

The respondents generally treated the books with religious content with respect. None of the respondents indicated they would sell or destroy the materials after they finished the program. Many said they would read the books again: eighty percent of the Muslims and sixty-eight point four percent of the Hindus said they would read the books again. Some respondents reported they would give the books to another use (twenty percent of Muslims and seventy point seven percent of Hindus). Some of the Hindus would keep the books but not read them again (thirteen point nine percent). The implication is that possibly more than fifty percent of participants may reread the primers.

Summary of Effects on Sociocultural and Religious Attitudes

Some movements in the cognitive, affective, and behavioral effects on the sociocultural and religious attitudes were a direct result of this literacy program among the Hindus and Muslims. Those who joined this program had specific educational goals that were practical to daily life, including not being cheated, use in daily life, and to teach their children.

Before joining the program, almost fifty percent of Hindus and Muslims had heard some of the stories, but over forty percent of Hindus and eighty percent of Muslims had never heard these stories before. Nearly eighty percent of Hindus and 100 percent of Muslims found the Bible stories practical for their lives. Over sixty percent of Hindus and eighty percent of Muslims would read the primers again. The responses indicated the Hindus and Muslims had an overall positive attitude toward the Bible stories used in this program.

The respondents did most of their learning in a group, not outside of class time. About forty percent indicated that they enjoyed the class and learned a lot.

CHAPTER 16

Other Dynamics and Effects of the Literacy Study

Other factors affected learning. These also influenced how the author offered the literary project, how it was received by participants, and its success.

Learning in a Group

Class dynamics is another factor in learning. Participants were asked, "Do you enjoy your literacy classes?" Respondents, asked who enjoyed the class, were split; forty one point one percent indicated "Sometimes" and forty-three point eight percent ticked "Always." This would imply that a little more than forty percent really enjoyed the class (see Figure 12).

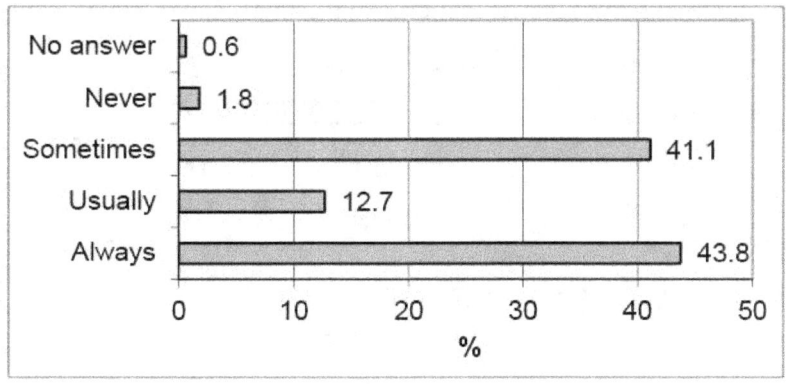

FIGURE 12 RESPONDENTS' ENJOYMENT OF THE CLASS

When asked, "How many hours in a day do you study your books outside of group time?" Some, nineteen point seven percent, had no time to study; point seven percent said that they studied more than four hours a day; point three percent said they studied three to four hours a day. The majority indicated that twenty-one point four percent studied one to two hours, and fifty-seven point nine studied less than one hour.

Participants were asked, "Do you review the lessons covered in each class outside of class on your own or with others?" A small number, point three percent, did not give an answer, while nine point four percent admitted that they never reviewed. Those who indicated that they sometimes reviewed their lessons was fifty-nine point two per cent. Those who usually reviewed their lessons were twelve percent, while nineteen point one percent reviewed their lessons daily. Therefore, most studying happened in the gathering time and not much outside it.

To follow up, they were asked, "Did you learn from these classes?" About forty percent of the respondents believed that they learned a lot from the program (see Figure 13).

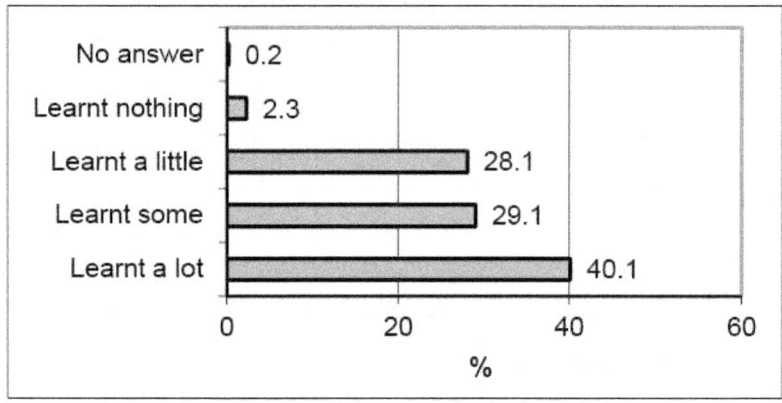

FIGURE 13 RESPONDENTS' LEVEL OF LEARNING FROM CLASSES

Literacy Effects

This section evaluates the reading and comprehension abilities of the respondents, excluding those who have secondary-level schooling, which make up ten percent of the sample. Those who were non-literate were not excluded from this sample because some (no more than three percent) became literate as a result of the program. Although the effects of the use of audio and print primarily increased reading and comprehension skills, a learner's writing and numeral skills were also influenced in this program.

Reading and comprehension evaluations were conducted on four levels. The first level evaluated their ability to read a sentence from the *Shukhobor* Set 1. The second level evaluated a sentence from *Shukhobor* Set 2, the third level took a sentence from the NRP Book 1, and the fourth level used a headline from a local Bengali newspaper.

Using the Cloze method of testing, respondents filled in the blanks to complete sentences from the four categories they read.

Three levels of writing assignments were given: write their name, their address, and a sentence to express their reason for joining the group. To check numeral skill, they answered a simple math problem requiring addition and subtraction. At the end of the evaluation, the respondents were asked what they thought of the above testing.

Effects on Reading Abilities

Table 18 compares the abilities of the respondents to read the different categories. Cross-referencing the demographics, twenty-three percent indicated that they were non-literate. Up to six percent had gained some literacy skills; the exit survey indicated that less than twenty-three percent were "Not able to read at all." In all categories of reading, less than fifty percent, but more that twenty-five percent, were able to read a whole sentence. These percentages decreased with increasing levels of reading difficulty. The implication of the reading results is promising. It shows an increase from the baseline and the results of reading tests from the pre-testing stages.

TABLE 18: READING ABILITIES OF RESPONDENTS

Passage read/ Evaluation	*Shukhobor* Set 1, Primer 1	*Shukhobor* Set 2, Primer 1	NRP Book 1	Newspaper headline
No answer	0.3%	0.0%	0.0%	0.0%
Not able to read at all	17.4%	20.1%	20.1%	21.4%
Able to read part of the sentence	29.8%	34.2%	32.4%	41.8%
Able to read the whole sentence	42.5%	35.7%	37.5%	26.8%

Effects on Comprehension Abilities

The Cloze test of comprehension was used in which the respondents were to fill in the blanks of alternate words to see if the respondents understood the meaning and structure of the sentence. Table 19 shows the results of the comprehension abilities in each reading category.

TABLE 19: COMPREHENSION ABILITIES OF RESPONDENTS

Passage read/ Evaluation	*Shukhobor* Set 1, Primer 1	*Shukhobor* Set 2, Primer 1	NRP Book 1	Newspaper headline
Not able to fill in the blanks	20.7%	23.7%	24.4%	29%
Able to fill in some of the blanks	39.8%	46.5%	43.5%	45.2%
Able to fill in all the blanks	29.5%	19.8%	22.1%	15.8%

Though reading skills increased, comprehension abilities did not increase proportionately. The implication is that more than forty percent have only partial understanding of the text; between fifteen and thirty percent had a complete understanding of what they read.

Effects on Writing and Math Abilities

Respondents were asked to write their names; and ninety-one point six percent could write their names. Half of those who had indicated that they were non-literate were able to do this. Next, respondents were asked to write their addresses, and seventy-two point two percent could write their addresses.

The respondents were asked to write a sentence giving a reason why they joined the literacy program. Nearly sixty-four percent could do so. These sentences were mostly short and sometimes repeated by individuals, but according to the UNESCO definition, sixty percent of the respondents met this standard for literacy.

Respondents were also given a simple math problem. The majority, eighty four percent, gave the right answer; ten percent gave a wrong answer; and about six percent had no answer. This revealed that some of the respondents could do simple mathematics.

At the end of the tests, the respondents were asked what they thought about the test. A small percentage gave no answer, nearly twenty-eight percent said it was difficult or very difficult. The remaining seventy-two percent said that it was easy.

Literacy Improvements of New Readers

Cross-tabulation of the reading and writing results was done with new readers. According to earlier information reported in the demographics, twenty-three point one percent were non-literate before joining the group, five point seven percent were taught by someone, two point seven percent were self-taught, and twenty one point percent had been in another adult education literacy group before joining this program. Adding these percentages together, fifty-three point two percent were new readers.

TABLE 20: CROSS-TABULATION OF READING *SHUKHOBOR* 1 WITH NEW READERS

Education prior to program	Read all	Read part	Could not read
Adult education literacy group	40.0%	41.5%	18.4%
Self-taught	25.0%	50.0%	25.0%
Taught by someone	5.9%	64.7%	29.4%
Non-literate before joining the program	27.5%	27.6%	44.9%

The first category was reading the primer from *Shukhobor* Set 1. This reading category, the easiest, had the best reading results. The cross tabulation shows that the "Could not read" category came from the whole spectrum of educational backgrounds, not only those who were non-literate.

TABLE 21: CROSS-TABULATION OF READING *SHUKHOBOR* 2 WITH NEW READERS

Education prior to program	Read all	Read part	Could not read
Adult education literacy group	27.7%	55.3%	16.9%
Self-taught	12.5%	62.5%	25.0%
Taught by someone	5.9%	35.3%	58.8%
Non-literate before joining the program	17.4%	37.7%	44.9%

The figures decreased of those who could read the whole sentence, and increased in the percentage who could read part of the sentence. The drop was between ten to twenty percent in the "Read all" category from the first reading evaluation to the second. There was an approximate drop of ten percent in reading abilities the "Read all" category from Table 20 to Table 21.

TABLE 22: CROSS-TABULATION OF READING NRP WITH NEW READERS

Education prior to program	Read all	Read part	Could not read
Adult education literacy group	26.2%	55.4%	18.5%
Self-taught	12.5%	62.5%	25.0%
Taught by someone	5.9%	35.3%	58.8%
Non-literate before joining the program	24.6%	29.0%	46.4%

The evaluation of the reading of *Shukhobor* 2 and the NRP showed nearly the same results (see Tables 21 and 22). This implied that the level of reading difficulty of these two types of printed materials was compatible. The target audience for this program was the first category of people who had been through adult education literacy classes. It was a pleasant surprise that those in the second category—the self-taught—also benefited: twelve point five percent could read the whole passage in both types of printed materials. In the last two categories, the educational foundations for those self-taught or taught by someone else were weak. However, twelve point five percent of the former could read the whole passage, and five point nine percent of the latter could read both types of printed materials. The most surprising results were from those who were non-literate before joining: seventeen point four percent could read *Shukhobor* 2, and twenty-four point six percent could read all of the NRP. It is difficult to explain why the second percentage is higher. Perhaps some participants were already familiar with the story of the wise and foolish builders and so could read this passage easily.

TABLE 23: CROSS-TABULATION OF READING NEWSPAPER HEADLINE WITH NEW READERS

Education prior to program	Read all	Read part	Could not read
Adult education literacy group	13.8%	63.1%	23.1%
Self-taught	0.0%	75.0%	25.0%
Taught by someone	5.9%	35.3%	58.8%
Non-literate before joining the program	17.4%	36.2%	46.4%

In the most difficult reading category, percentages of reading abilities dropped drastically. This implies that there is still a big difference from materials written for new readers and those written for the general educated adult population.

TABLE 24: CROSS-TABULATION OF WRITING AND DOING MATH WITH NEW READERS

Education level prior to program	Write name	Write address	Write sentence	Solve math problem
Adult education literacy group	92.3%	69.2%	60.0%	81.5%
Self-taught	87.5%	87.5%	37.5%	12.5%
Taught by someone	100.0%	41.2%	17.6%	17.6%
Non-literate before joining the program	73.9%	42.0%	36.2%	13.0%

In all categories of reading, writing, and solving math problems, the results from those who were non-literate before joining the program is impressive. The implication is that some of the respondents value writing, as well as being able to do simple mathematics.

Summary of the Literacy Effects

There are definite literacy effects on the users as a direct result of the program. The average reading skill from the easiest to the hardest reading categories of those respondents being able to read the whole sentence was between forty to twenty percent. However, comprehension abilities did not correspond with reading abilities. The difference between those able to read the whole sentence and fill in all the blanks in the Cloze test was approximately ten percent.

The program may have served to impact the respondents' writing abilities, although some of them were able to write their names and addresses before coming to the program. It is estimated that fifteen to sixty percent improved their ability to write sentences.

CHAPTER 17

Analysis of Distribution and Supervision

After producing the materials, it was important to market them in ways that the materials would be used properly. Below are responses from supervisors and church leaders who were involved in the distribution and supervision of the program.

Use of the Literacy Materials

Insights on how the materials had been used were gleaned from questionnaires and interviews conducted with the supervisors and the church leaders. Responses to the question, "In what ways would you use these materials?" were:

- in a literacy program.
- sell them to people to earn revenue.
- for educating the people so that they can read the Scriptures.
- use them for Bible study.
- use them in a program with a health emphasis.

These materials may have multiple uses beyond a literacy program. In fact, it might be a more holistic and effective strategy to couple it with other programs.

The two tracks of literacy materials were developed for two different uses. Pastors were polled about how they used the two tracks. These results are recorded in Table 25. There was a split opinion on whether *Shukhobor* could be used for evangelism and church planting. There was stronger support for *Muktir Path* as discipleship material but less support for its use as a Bible study. There was a stronger agreement that *Shukhobor* is purely educational and, interestingly, the pastors thought that *Muktir Path* could be used with non-Christians as well. Likewise, they thought that *Shukhobor* should be used inside the church. They saw *Muktir Path* as good Bible introductory materials. They were split on the theological soundness of both the materials. This issue may need to be tested in the future: what does that mean and how can it be corrected if necessary? Both sets of materials need careful evaluation, using the pastors' comments to improve the content.

TABLE 25: OTHER USES OF THE LITERACY MATERIALS

	Disagree	Slightly Agree	Agree	Strongly Agree
Shukhobor is good for evangelism.	20%	20%	30%	30%
Muktir Path is good for discipleship.	10%	20%	20%	50%
Shukhobor can be used for church planting.	20%	10%	40%	20%
Muktir Path can be used for Bible study.	20%	10%	40%	20%
Shukhobor can be used for purely educational purposes.	30%	10%	20%	40%
Muktir Path can only be used with Christians.	40%	10%	30%	20%
Shukhobor can only be used outside of the church.	40%	30%	10%	20%

Muktir Path is good Bible introductory material.	20%	10%	40%	30%
Shukhobor is theologically sound.	40%	10%	20%	30%
Muktir Path is theologically sound.	40%	10%	20%	30%

Supervision of the Program

Supervisors managed groups in Gopalganj, Mymensingh, Greater Rajshahi, and Birganj. All of them supervised more than five groups. They visit each group more than twelve times in a year. They indicated that they had a good grasp of their responsibilities to:

- Stay in touch with the members of each group.
- Keep close communication with the pastors or church leaders.
- Motivate the facilitator.
- Spiritually motivate members and the facilitator.
- Give practical assistance.
- If facilitators encounter problems, offer solutions.
- Distribute the materials.

The church leaders, on the other hand, suggested how this program could be conducted more effectively:

- Half of the salary provided by the Bible Society and half by the church, so that supervision was done well, with shared interests.
- A basic literacy program that could be put under the social development arm of the church.
- Materials available in local tribal languages.
- More training for the facilitator after completion of each set of materials.
- Good to meet with the supervisors twice a month.

- Frequent checks on the learners' writing progress.
- Frequent checks on the learners' reading progress.
- The 20 percent drop-out rate could be due to the 5-day-a-week class system, which is too taxing for students.
- Give no examinations or evaluations.
- Reward facilitators who are volunteers with some honorarium.
- Solicit benefits from government and NGOs for literacy groups, including lamps, pens, notebooks, and facilities.

Many suggestions revolved around the Bible Society contributing more money and resources to the program. Not much was said about their own increased commitment and contribution of finances and personnel.

Follow-up Programs

Follow-up programs are strategic for any literacy plan. Supervisors and church leaders were polled as to how these programs should be conducted. These suggestions were given by supervisors as to how to follow up with group members:

- Motivation seminars.
- Prizes for those who complete the materials.
- Consultation meetings with pastors to do follow-up.
- Continuing direction for the group.
- Ongoing access to audio products by group. These were suggestions from church leaders on how to effectively follow up on the group members.
- Annual conference for participants.
- Three to six months ongoing reviews of the lessons, with updates on how members are doing.
- Encourage learners to sing the program songs, even in church services.
- Encourage learners to read the books by themselves.

- Personal follow-up of group members by facilitators.
- Home meetings.

The follow-up suggestions could help new readers to take their literacy skills a step further so that they do not lapse back into non-literacy. Past literacy programs show that efforts for literacy training can be in vain if the participants are not motivated and there are no new avenues for practical use of their literacy skills.

Summary of the Analysis of Distribution and Supervising System

Supervisors and church leaders perceived that these materials could be used along with other development programs such as health and savings. The church leaders were split about how to use these materials. It might be helpful to evaluate these materials for their use in evangelism, discipleship, Bible study, and education programs. Other criteria helpful for evaluations would be the appropriateness of their use inside and outside the church, and theological soundness.

The supervisors had a good understanding of their job. Church leaders suggested that the cost be carried more by the Bible Society than the local church. They suggested follow-up programs such as holding more classes, so that the learner will not lose their literacy skills.

CHAPTER 18

The Impact of the Literacy Program on Local Churches

ON LOCAL CHURCHES

The literacy program was conducted in cooperation with the local churches. Local churches were the contact points in the villages, as well as the providers of personnel. Church leaders often formed the supervising committees so that the field supervisors and facilitators were accountable for their work to a local committee. These committees also served as advisory boards when the groups encountered difficulties.

Number of Groups Formed under Each Church

Table 26 shows the number of groups formed under each church from 1996-1999.

TABLE 26: CHURCHES INVOLVED IN THE LITERACY PROGRAM

Church Name/Denomination		Church supervision	Involved Nov. 1998-Oct. 1999	Total per Church
Assemblies of God Church	2	4	-	6
ABWE Church	-	5	-	5
B. Baptist Church	1	-	14	15
B. Baptist Fellowship	3	5	-	8
Church of Bangladesh	3	-	-	3
Eternal Holiness Church	-	2	-	2

Fellowship Church	1	-	-	1
Full Gospel Church	-	3	-	3
Garo Baptist Convention	1	-	-	1
Lutheran Church (BLC)	-	40	-	40
Lutheran Church (BENLC)	1	-	-	1
Nazarene Church	-	-	7	7
Seventh Day Adventist Church	2	18	-	20
Talitha Koumi Church	1	7	7	15
TOTAL	15	84	28	127

Descriptions of Selected Churches

The Bangladesh Methodist Church was established in 1984 and currently has 185 churches with a membership of 18,698 (http://worldmethodistcouncil.org/about/memberchurches/name/bangladesh-methodist-church/(accessed February 15, 2020)). Methodist churches are located in different parts of Bangladesh. Other denominational activities include a seminary and schools. Since the literacy program is an extra program, they suggested that the BBS share in half the payment of facilitators. The Methodist Bishop was the second vice-chairman of BBS board.

The Assemblies of God was established in Bangladesh in the early 1960s. They have 400 churches and a membership of more than 40,000. According to their General Superintendent, they have four separate district councils. Other programs under this denomination include 55 free primary schools.

The Church of the Nazarene was established in 1993. There were five districts with churches. Other denominational programs include community health care (http://prod.nazarene.org/article/denomination-establishes-2-new-bangladesh-districts(accessed February 15, 2020)).

The Seventh Day Adventist Church (SDA) was established in 1948 and has 120 churches and 30,000 members (https://news.adventist.org/en/all-news/news/go/2018-0316/bangla-deshadventists-offerhealtheducation-for-muslimcaregivers(accessed February15, 2020)). Other programs in this denomination include schools, a high school in each section, a college and university, and an outreach through English schools. Scholarships for schooling are given on the basis of faithfulness in the church. There are also health and dental clinics. The SDA had 19 literacy groups in partnership with BBS. Salaried schoolteachers facilitated the literacy program. The groups are mixed in gender and religion.

The Garo Baptist Convention was established in 1890, and has 157 churches with a membership of 12,850 (https://www.bwanet.org/statistics(accessed February 15, 2020)). These churches are located near the Indian border in Mymensingh district where the majority of the Garo tribes reside. Other programs under this denomination include clinics, hospitals, and a credit program.

The Presbyterian Fellowship of Bangladesh was established in 1980. They are involved in church planting and evangelism. The church was not able to pay the facilitators and are presently having volunteers run the program as a ministry.

The Bangladesh Baptist Church is the oldest Protestant denomination in Bangladesh. There are 374 churches. BBS worked with the church in Kaligram that was started in 1839. BBS had two groups under this denomination.

The BLC was established in 1979 and has a registered membership of 6,270 adult persons (https://www.luth-eranworld.org/content/bangladesh-lutheran-church(accessed February 15, 2020)). This church was closely associated with the Danish Santal Mission that managed other development projects.

New Converts as a Result of the Program

The church leaders were asked if there were any converts from the program. Only the SDA mentioned converts from the program. There were 30 newly baptized SDA members in Jessore. These converts were Hindus and Muslims of both genders.

Observable Changes in Church Members

The church leaders thought that the program was useful to their church members. These were the comments as to how they felt that this program had impacted their church members.

- Church members who volunteered as facilitators believed they were doing evangelism.
- Church members learned new songs.
- Church members understood the Bible stories.
- The children of church members benefited from their parents being able to read.
- The members became interested in religious programs and regular church attendance increased.
- The members could sing for themselves.
- The members could read the books from the program for themselves.
- The members know the Good News.
- The members had a deeper knowledge of the Bible.
- The prayer lives of church members deepened.
- The members regularly joined church services and programs Supervisors observed these changes in church members as a direct result of the literacy program.
- Spiritual life of members increased by participation in fasting, church attendance, and changes in personal lifestyles.
- Members remembered what the pastor said, Bible stories, and songs.
- Members improved their writing and reading.
- Members formed a savings group.
- Members were sharing Christ with their neighbors.
- Members read the Bible and sang songs.
- Members were drinking less wine.
- Members continued to go to church.
- Giving in church offerings by members had increased.

Observable Changes among Group Members

Supervisors mentioned these changes in behavior among group members:

- Hindus and Muslims in the group became positive towards Christians.

- Their relationships with each other were good.
- They learned from *Shukhobor* that they should behave well with those from other religions.
- They respected each other and were not quarreling.

Summary of the Impact of the Literacy Programs on the Local Churches

The literacy program made a definite impact on the local church. This program expanded in a short period, from initial BLC groups to 13 other denominations. The sample of respondents came from eight denominations: Methodist, Assemblies of God, Church of the Nazarene, SDA, Garo Baptist Convention, Presbyterian Fellowship, Bangladesh Baptist Church, and the BLC.

The program was not used for evangelism except by the SDA. However, there were observable positive changes in church members, as well as in Hindus and Muslims who joined the program.

CHAPTER 19

Contextualizing the Literacy Project

From the onset of the research process, an emerging pattern indicated the need for the use of mixed media. Baseline research showed that the conventional literacy method was ineffective in sustaining literacy or for leading more than ten percent of participants to functional literacy. This baseline information also provided factors that affected learners. Issues included physical tiredness, social relationships, and elements in literacy training, such as a practical curriculum, good teachers, length and frequency of the course, as well as follow-up visits by supervisors.

This baseline information led to an opportunity to experiment and develop a system with a media-mix of audio and print. The first set of materials for general use in villages was called *Shukhobor* Set 1. The program yielded motivation, some improvement in reading with comprehension during a limited test period, and the possible effectiveness of communication of Scripture.

In the two years between July 1995 and June 1997, the materials were used by the BLC under BLM-D, in a geographic area with a BLC congregation. By the end of two years, reading with comprehension results increased, with indications of functional literacy by some participants.

The most recent field research in 2000 compared participants who began the program in 1996 through 1997. The demographic sketch showed that the respondents in this sample were over the age of fifteen, a little more than seventy percent were women, eighty percent were married, and a little more than seventy-five percent were housewives and day-laborers. About seventy-two percent were Christian, twenty-six percent were Hindu and about two percent were Muslim. A small percentage of participants from tribal groups (Paharis, Santalis, and Garos from Mymensingh, Rajshahi, Bogra, Dinajpur, Nilphamari, and Gopalganj) were included in the sample. Half of the respondents had formal education and the other half did not. About fifty-eight percent of the respondents were from the most recent groups of 1999; the rest were from earlier groups (1996 through 1998).

This survey indicates positive effects on knowledge, attitudes and behavior of the respondents in learning to read, motivation and a deepened understanding of the Bible and Christianity. The positive effects in the last two categories were true among the Hindus and Muslims since the program exposed them to the Bible and Christianity.

During the three years of the program, between twenty-five and thirty percent of the respondents could functionally read an NRP passage and a newspaper headline. A high percentage could write their names, their addresses, and a sentence, as well as solve a math problem. Although many participants had more formal education than allowed by the research design, about fifty percent were new readers.

In the analysis of the use, supervision, and follow-up program of the literacy materials, the supervisors and church leaders gave some helpful suggestions. Descriptions of main denominations involved with this program were given. Except for the Seventh Day Adventist church, other churches did not report on any conversions as a result of this program. However, church leaders and supervisors expressed that they thought that the program had positive effects on the spiritual lives and Christian behavior of church members.

The development of the entire project in Bangladesh is unique to the context of that country. To successfully adapt this literacy program in other countries, the program has to be contextualized accordingly. It would be unwise to merely duplicate what was done in one context and expect it to work successfully in another, without necessary adjustments to make that program acceptable in a new context.

Seven recurring contextual factors formed the conceptual framework for the adaptation of this program into other cultural contexts: history, religion, sociopolitical situation, arts, education, media, and ecclesiastical involvement. In the following sections each of the contextual factors from a theoretical perspective with a broad base of application will be discussed. Both positive and negative aspects of how each contextual factor has actually influenced, or bears the potential to influence, the development of the program in Bangladesh will be examined. Finally, a series of adaptation questions as an aid for adaptation in a different context will be provided. Since these contextual factors do overlap with one another, in referring to one, we may refer to others.

Historical Context

The past informs the present and the future, and in any specific country and context, the past in relation to literacy should also be considered. History narrates what happened in a past time, place, and environment from the present standpoint of the historian. The potential pitfall lies in whether the researcher is able to maintain objectivity, seek the truth of historical events, and discern important facts, as well as any bias or tainted information seen from a particularly slanted viewpoint of the historian. Since the 1960s, historical research has been done using the disciplines and perspectives of social science, women's history, and cultural history to guide the information gathering. However, amidst these "new histories" empirical and rational analysis is still applied. Data and information are analyzed in order to ensure the trustworthiness of sources (Munslow 2001:n.p.).

General Historical Influences

Each country has its own rich historical heritage, and the historical past of a country in relation to literacy serves as a springboard for a literacy program to be appreciated. For example, in China, the classical books of Chinese culture are clearly defined and have a steady readership. However, after the revolution of 1949, books lost their charm as the government used them as tools for propaganda. Another example is the country of Japan that has a tradition of literacy extending back well over a millennium. Similar to the Chinese situation, classical Japanese books make up a cultural canon, forming a body of knowledge that imparts an identity and continuity to the Japanese culture (Kenji 2000:n.p.).

The counterpoint is that some studies indicate that the abilities to adapt and learn are not dependent on literacy skills. In a study of the Vai people, a small West African group who invented their own writing system, tests were conducted with 1,000 participants. Subjects included geometric sorting tasks, logic tests, and categorizing. Among the participants were non-literates, those literate in Vai, Arabic or both scripts, as well as those schooled in English. The results did not prove conclusively that a literate person is better educated than a non-literate person (Brilla 1998:n.p.).

Literacy history shows that no one literacy approach is perfect. Instead, a combination of different elements, such as the community-base model of Freire, the discipleship model of Laubach, and the whole language learning of Gudschinsky make a program more efficient. Other models may be even more effective than the ones mentioned here.

Historical research should be done on each country's appreciation of literacy. Most countries have some historical background as to the development of their own language and writing systems. This information will inform, or guide, an adaptation process and, even if this history is transmitted orally, it would be helpful to use the stories. In fact, this oral tradition will help the development of these audio element materials. History can also motivate people of a country to appreciate their heritage of literacy gained from those who have gone before them.

Historical Influences on the Development of the Literacy Program

The Bangladesh people come from a long tradition of literacy and literature. They are proud of their language and mark it annually on February 21, the day of the Language Movement of 1952. The United Nations adopted this day as Language Day internationally. This history of language strengthens the need for literacy training and programs because of the pride Bangladeshis have for their language.

Starting from the Mogul era to the occupation of Pakistan, the people of Bangladesh fought for survival, and to hold on to their rich cultural heritage, particularly language. The British tried to impose

English on the Bangladeshis but many refused to learn it. Pakistanis wanted them to use Urdu as the main language, but Bangladeshis protested to the point of bloodshed. This pride in their language has made the Bangladeshis a resilient and strong people, but it has had negative effects as well. Their lack of a strong base in the English language has rendered them less competitive on the world scene where English is the *lingua franca*. Their refusal to consent to making Urdu their national language caused the separation with Pakistan.

The first full Bible translation in Bengali can be traced back to William Carey. It is unfortunate that most people today are not familiar with the high literary Bengali used in this translation. This literary language used is archaic—some of it already obsolete in modern Bengali—and is Sanskrit-based in contrast to modern Bengali, which is Arabic-based. Even some of the highly-educated Bengalis have serious difficulty in understanding the old language fully. The Carey version has been the main Bible translation printed by the Bible Society, but in recent years new translations have been completed to make the Bible more readable and understandable.

The mandate that the United Bible Societies has set for themselves compels them to look at literacy. In their history in this area, they attempted to meet the need by providing simple reading materials using a translation of the New Reader Portions but this did not achieve the objective of ensuring that new readers could read the portions. The BBS even formed cassette teams that took the Word out to the people using audio products. Their purpose was to form listening groups, as well as to market audio Scriptures. Aside from producing a variety of audio scriptural products for different audiences, the major project has been the production of literacy materials. The latest strategy has been to promote a literacy program using audio Scriptures along with primers.

The program in Bangladesh builds upon the pride that Bangladeshis have in their language. In one instance, there were protests on the publication of the Bible translation using more Islamic-Muslim terminology. However, scholarly literary Muslim professors defended the translation for its literary value.

Adaptation Questions on Historical Context

Adaptation questions that should be asked about the historical context are:

- What is the general history of the context?
- How can this history be used to understand the cultural context?
- How does the history of the country relate to literacy?
- What can be learned from history regarding the acceptance of the Scriptures and their use in literacy programs?
- How can this history be motivational for people and create a positive reception to a Scripture-based literacy program?

Religious Context

Religion is culturally universal and every culture has customs, belief systems, myths, as well as power relations built around religious orientations. These customs are often expressed in rituals that act out beliefs that often correspond to seasonal matters, such as planting and harvest. Other customs and beliefs include contingencies such as life crises, avoidance of affliction, initiation or entrance into a new stage or group, defense of self or community, and acknowledgment of spirits and good fortune (Turner 1973:1,104). The influence of religion in a person's life cannot be overestimated. Almost every member of any community participates in religion as they join the rituals or adhere to the religious philosophy.

General Religious Influences

Judaism, Islam, and Christianity uphold a holy book and their adherents are known as "people of the Book." These adherents are motivated to learn to read because the desire to read the Bible, the Quran, the Torah, or other religious books for themselves. With Hinduism and Buddhism, and even less with animism, there is less emphasis on written words. Communication is more in terms of symbolism and practice.

Wayne Leman, a Bible translator writes:

> It seems to me that much of our desire to be "people of the Book" is good, but because we are human, and that means being fallible, we allow the good focus upon the written Word to become something, over time, that misses the priority focus of our lives, which should be to honor God and share the Good News with others that he has a free gift, a way for humans to be acceptable to him. . . . Does translating for Bibleless tribes equate with "giving them the Word"? . . . If we do not help them have the tools needed to translate that Word into life, then it is not a complete translation process (nd:n.p.).

The availability of the Bible is such that everyone who wants to can have access to it (Swim 2002:n.p.). The struggle of the Reformation was about putting the Bible into the hands of all people. Wycliffe Bible Translators have made giant steps forward in Bible translation, with more than 2,000 languages having some portion of Scripture translated (Wycliffe Bible Translators nd.:n.p.). Church leaders encourage literacy so that people can read the Bible for themselves.

The support of religious leaders for literacy is invaluable. Religious leaders influence people in their particular religion; followers look to the leaders for guidance and counsel. For example, the success of one literacy program was because the Islamic teachers, the *imams* and *mullahs*, were persuaded of the importance of literacy. They allowed literacy classes to be conducted in their own courtyards (Joydhor 2000).

Religious Influences on the Development of the Literacy Program

The baseline research survey done in Bangladesh affirmed that respondents wanted to read good stories. What better stories than Bible stories (Chai 2000:43). Thus, the *Shukhobor* set of literacy materials was developed to expose new readers to Scriptures, with the focused intent of increasing literacy skills. This valid entry point into any religious and secular environment will provide in-roads to people by creating a positive climate toward the gospel. This does not imply the need to compromise by using material from other religions, but it does require sensitivity in presentation.

The BBS pre-tested the first *Shukhobor* set using the *Muslimani*[1] Bible translations. They could not have any illustrations in the primer of Jesus as this was offensive to the Muslim audience. Bible Society representatives asked permission of local Muslim leaders if they could do the literacy pre-test in their area and were met with a warm welcome. In fact, two of the groups met in the courtyards of these esteemed Muslim leaders, indicating their patronage and support of the program (Joydhor 2000).

The Bible stories chosen had secular themes of saving money, having good relationships with neighbors, and good farming. This need approach to Scripture selection also increased the reception of the *Shukhobor* series.

Leaders of all the religions were approached first for permission before starting the program in their immediate area. The content of the materials was not hidden from them, so the leaders were not deceived. They knew that the materials were with Bible stories with the intent of improving literacy in the participants. They gave an assurance of their support before the program was implemented. Church leaders were enthusiastic in their support and requested that the programs be implemented in their churches (Chai 2000:21).

Adaptation Questions on Religious Context

The adaptation questions that can be asked in applying this principle of working with the religious environment are:

- What are the dominant religions in the country?
- What religious materials do people want to read?
- Who are the key people within the context who can assist in motivating and encouraging people to participate in the literacy program?

---

[1] This is a Bible translation that uses Arabic terms.

- How can there be sensitivity in presentation without compromising the use of Scriptures?
- Which Bible passages can address the needs of the people?

Sociopolitical Context

Social and political pressures are real in people's lives. Though people are individuals, they are also a part of social groups based on geographical location, racial identity, or even family ties. A more structured form of power lies in the political arena, where policies and laws are made that influence a country. Sociopolitical development is the process of organizing human beings and directing their energies as well as activities toward achieving higher levels of results in all aspects of public life (Jacobs and Cleveland 1999:n.p.).

General Sociopolitical Influences

Pressure from peers cannot be overestimated, as peers can discourage a person who may really want to learn. Such people would rather not learn than be ridiculed by their community. However, the literacy program provides a social gathering for human beings to connect with each other as they have a common need and goal. It provides a time and place to escape the mundane life of hard work and family challenges and to have a short respite to study and do something completely different. We are all social beings in a larger group and society. This sociological norm should be respected and adhered to so that one can be nurtured in a safe, familiar place, rather than a foreign setting. Strength can be found in numbers, and the group dynamics encourage each individual to strive towards a better life as each helps the other to succeed. Many of the countries with great literacy needs are also socially oriented societies. Forming groups for literacy would be relatively easy in such settings.

If politicians see that promoting literacy can be to their advantage, laws and policies will be passed accordingly. For example, many developing countries reap the benefits from UNESCO, or the World Bank, because theirs is a humanitarian cause. Illiteracy is placed on the list of evils that must be eradicated. Unfortunately, no eradication has happened; instead, laws that prohibit literacy or educational programs have been implemented, as in some strict Islamic countries that do not allow females to be educated (The World Bank Group 1998:n.p.).

Sociopolitical Influences on the Development of the Literacy Program

Visits to literacy groups in Bangladesh show that these classes are also social gatherings. Women and men meet in safe and common spaces. People of different religions can gather to learn together. Differences can be laid aside and commonality is emphasized with the shared goal of improving literacy skills. Each participant may discuss, and contribute to each other's learning, on equal terms. There is an atmosphere of joy and having fun as they joke and tease each other without being hurtful or unkind. The songs that they sing together and the stories they share create a healthy bond between human beings who share the hardship of life together (Chai 2000:33).

Political leaders have power of influence over their followers and supporters, but opinion leaders in a community also exercise a profound amount of influence. I have personally encountered an opinion leader in Nilphamari, the small town where I stayed in northwestern Bangladesh. He was the owner of a food supplies shop and also functioned like a local judge. His opinion was much sought after in matters of civil dispute. Often he provided the resolution. Although he was not a visible political leader, he was highly regarded and respected by his community, and thus possessed the power of influence on the people around him. He is a learned man, self-taught, and skilled in Bengali, Arabic, and English. He encouraged his constituency to join our literacy groups to become literate. It is important to have the support of both political and opinion leaders (Chai 2000:41).

Adaptation Questions of the Sociopolitical Context

The adaptation questions that can be asked of the sociopolitical influences would be:

- What are the sociopolitical structures in the society?
- Which sociopolitical laws and policies affect a literacy program?
- What is the status of women in the context?
- How can classes be a social gathering that are contextually acceptable?
- How can opinion leaders be persuaded to be supportive of a Scripture-focused and media-based literacy program?

Artistic Context

The arts have the power to move people to revolution or to revelation—or both simultaneously. The arts touch human emotions and intellect in a deep way, as art is the product of the act of creating. It is closely linked to the fact that human beings are created and there is a Creator. These acts of creating involve at least three major aspects: environment, thought processes, and cultural heritage. The true artist uses intellect to change environment and cultural heritage. As art develops, cultural heritage increases in complexity, gearing a human being towards spiritual matters and expressions in more abstract forms of art involving personal concepts of beauty and love (Bowman 2002:n.p.).

General Artistic Influences

Music can calm people and set a mood for the environment. In literacy, music can motivate and put the learner in the mood to learn. Song lyrics can speak of the benefits of literacy, as the song stays in the minds and the hearts of the listeners longer than any lecture on the subject.

Drama takes an audience to another place and another time, and yet can bring across to its audience the intended message of the realities of life. In drama communicated predominantly via audio, the mind becomes the theater. The best dramas are contextualized. In Chiangmai, Thailand, a drama troupe performs Thai traditional drama called *ligae*. In one performance, they use the "Prodigal Daughter" instead of "son," because in Thailand it is often the girls who are given into prostitution and go to the city (Asian Institute of Christian Communication 2002).

The phrase "a picture is worth a thousand words" summarizes the value of illustrations. As Ane Haaland writes, "There is a belief among some people that even if a picture is bad, it will be better than not having a picture at all. . . . The argument against this belief is—why teach with a bad picture if you can teach with a good one?" (1984:54). Words and pictures can complement each other. Color is another emotive tool that carries different meanings in different cultures. In some cultures, black clothes are a sign of mourning but in others, as in the Indian subcontinent, widows wear white *sarees* and shave off all their hair. Yet in other cultures, white is the color of a wedding dress, too. Attractive well-combined colors bring a picture to life, though black and white pictures are not to be underestimated. For example, the Annie Voulton cartoons in the Good News Bibles (line drawings) depict the meaning of biblical stories in an excellent manner. Outstanding results can also be achieved by the use of light and shadow as a technique in black and white pictures (United Bible Societies 2000).

The well-known power of language is as old as an old Chinese proverb: "a six-inch tongue can cut down a six-foot person." The book of James speaks about the same tongue that can bless and curse. Language comes from the heart that wants to understand and be understood. Though language is neutral in itself, the same words in different contexts can either motivate or bear negative effects. It is an important vehicle for the transmission of ideas and information and the expression of poetry, stories, and proverbs.

God is not against culture. He allows us to use culture appropriately to communicate Scriptural truth. Some Christians stay away from cultural expressions, considering them demonic. Although this is an extreme opinion, not all cultural forms are acceptable either. A process of discernment can determine which aspects are appropriate, biblically acceptable, and useful to communicate Scriptures and teach literacy in the literacy program.

Artistic Influences on the Development of the Literacy Program

In literacy groups in Bangladesh, one of the highlights of the learning programs was singing Scripture-in-songs together. Some groups displayed musical talents by playing on hand-pump organs, drums, and cymbals. Some did impromptu dramas. Others could recite famous poetry from memory. In conversation, they incorporated appropriate proverbs that expressed their meaning without even noticing the beauty of the language that they were using.

The Scriptures-in-song used in the Bible Society literacy materials are original songs based on the Bible stories, sometimes set to popular tunes. This made learning the songs, and remembering the lyrics, easy. These songs were upbeat and encouraged an atmosphere of joy and goodwill (Joydhor 1999).

Illustrations used in the primer combined locally drawn pictures and Bible story clipart provided by the UBS. These carefully-selected pictures illustrated the story with local flavor, so that Bangladeshis in the village could identify with what was being portrayed. Each primer was color-coded for quick reference. For example, all *Shukhobor* sets began with a red book as the first, green as the second, purple as the third, and yellow as the fourth. This corresponded with the audio product jackets and plastic bags, which packaged all the materials together. Bold colors made the materials look attractive.

Adaptation Questions on Artistic Context

Adaptation questions that should be asked about art forms are:

- What are the popular art forms?
- What music would set the mood for learning?
- What drama would convey the message of Bible stories and literacy?
- Which illustrations and colors would effectively communicate Bible stories and literacy concepts?
- What language forms should be used to communicate with adult new readers?

Educational Context

People learn in different ways. Some use the right side of the brain (leaning toward linear thinking) more, while others use the left (non-linear thinking). In classrooms or academic groups, linear thinking is often forced upon people for whom it is not their preferred mode of learning. It is important to know the best way people of different cultures learn since different cultures often have a tendency to use either the left or right side of the brain while learning. For example, some African American students in public school may have a hard time learning in the traditional way in the public schooling of North America. Experimentation in more unconventional ways to teach these students, such as using rap music, increased discussion, and hands-on teaching methods may produce better academic results (https://africanamericancultureslp.weebly.com/learning-styles.html (accessed February 15, 2020)).

A person's learning style is a key educational concepts. For example, visual learners need to see to learn. They may think in pictures or learn best from visual displays like diagrams, illustrated textbooks, overhead transparencies, videos, flip-charts and hand-outs. An auditory learner learns best through lectures, discussions, verbalizing their thoughts, and listening to others. They often benefit from reading aloud and using a tape recorder. Tactile or kinesthetic persons learn best with a hands-on approach, actively exploring the physical world around them (Bogod n.d.:n.p.). Linguistic learners acquire information by reading, writing, and telling stories. Logical learners enjoy logical exercises like math problems. Spatial learners, similar to visual learners, learn by working with colors and pictures. Musical learners learn through music. Bodily learners, like kinesthetic, hands-on learners, need an active education. Interpersonal learners learn best through social interaction, while intrapersonal learners learn best on their own. People usually have a combination of these learning styles with one or more being dominant (Mantle 2001:n.p.).

General Educational Influences

This educational theory was built on the following eight concepts as proposed by Vygotsky and reported by Mary Ellen Goldfarb (2000:n.p.). These were value, knowledge, human nature, learning, transmission, society, opportunity, and consensus.

First, the learner must be convinced that knowledge and skills are worthwhile learning. Knowledge within a discipline is important, but the application of knowledge enables students to solve problems so that they can build new knowledge. Education helps human beings act to improve the human situation.

Second, education should emphasize intellectual development, not just increasing knowledge. Interaction between a culture's thought and language is the agent of change that leads to the development of higher thinking. "Thought and language, which reflect reality in a way different from that of perception, are the key to human consciousness" (Piaget 1932:n.p.).

Third, human beings are not limited to their biological inheritance, but are born into an environment, which has been shaped by the activities of previous generations. They are able to assimilate the experiences of others and continue to develop the capacity of intelligence.

Fourth, learning is a constructive activity. Language is a crucial tool in the cognitive process of determining how a person will learn to think. When a person wants to learn more, new words are demanded. Play is also a factor in acquiring skills and knowledge.

Fifth, instructors must be aware of progress in the learners' development. Knowledge and skills are best transferred when practical application is involved and the curriculum has relevance to life.

Sixth, social forces and social changes cause changes in human interactions and expectations. Society provides the place in which its members learn to think and develop their intelligences. Society shapes thought.

Seventh, many populations are non-literate because they lack an opportunity for education. It is not necessarily due to the lack of motivation or intelligence.

Eighth, a human being does not develop in isolation, but reacts to changes in the environment. Consensus forms society over time, where thoughts, actions, and experiences are culturally mediated.

The practical application of this educational theory lies in preparing literacy materials usable by the intended audience. The materials have not been taught if the learner has not learned. The burden of communication lies with the one from whom the message originates, and not the receptor to whom it is going. In order to communicate, the learner, or receptor, must always be the focus.

Four important questions from Søgaard help determine receptor orientation and cultural sensitivity (2001:3-4):

- Who is my listener?
- Where is my listener?
- What are the needs of my listener?
- How can I meet the needs of my listener?

The answers to these questions can determine the creation of effective materials.

The materials for adult literacy are being prepared for adults who have already experienced life and its stages. Therefore, the content of the materials should be meaningful to them. If the content to be learned has no immediate and real value, the adult learner will most likely reject the curriculum and not much learning will happen. The goal of the curriculum is both to teach a person how to read and, in the process, communicate information that is needed for living.

Stories and examples should be culturally appropriate or relevant. It is inappropriate to talk about snow in a place where it does not snow, or to refer to food such as hot dogs and hamburgers with people who have no idea what these are. Illustrations and concepts based on familiar things can communicate new ideas.

Educational Influences on the Development of the Literacy Program

The adaptation of this program should include a supporting educational system that is receptor-oriented and caters to those adult learners whose thinking is non-linear. This system should use research about cultural learning styles, an effective distribution system, and ongoing evaluation. In this way, the program will not become obsolete and ineffective.

In Bangladesh, the *Shukhobor* materials were built on the felt needs of the people. It dealt with practical topics such as the need for literacy, relationships with family and neighbors, and farming. Culturally appropriate dramatic and musical presentations emphasized the main teaching point. People were not brought into classrooms to sit on chairs but sat cross-legged in the light of an oil lamp in their own courtyards, in the open air, or in stables.

The Bible Society designed the literacy materials for a group setting, as well as for individuals. The materials included audio and visual elements—the audio product and the primer. Exercises included reading aloud into the tape recorder and written exercises in the primer. The primary emphasis was upon gaining reading skills, but writing and mathematical elements were also included.

Adaptation Questions on Educational Systems

Adaptation questions that can be asked of the educational context to create a receptor-oriented educational system are:

- How do these people learn?
- What are their felt needs?
- How can the curriculum address those felt needs?
- What are the best places and times for learning to take place?
- What educational activities would be effective in creating a learning situation?

Media Context

The communication revolution, marked by the synergy of satellites, computers and digitalization, affects every country so that today's reality is an electronic projection of the real world. There has been a global paradigm shift influenced by the advent of revolutionary information and communications technology. This shift has changed the content and the context of international politics. This context includes anyone who is connected to, and affected by, media. Information and communication technology is helping to avoid many levels of bureaucracy that limit access to information (Pathania 2002:n.p.). South Asia seems to have belatedly understood the nature of the global economic reality. Many South Asian countries suffer from widespread illiteracy, which is a clear obstacle to entering the information highway. These countries must leapfrog into a communication revolution and improve access to traditional mass media like newspapers, radio, television, and cinema, while catching up with other countries who are technologically advanced (Pathania 2002:n.p.).

Fran Trampiets (2000:1), cautions against the fast pace of media's influences. When dealing with print media, we can adjust our reading speed and level of attention to our purpose for reading. We can take time to analyze and reflect on the words, relate them to personal experience and prior knowledge, and decide if we agree or disagree with the statements. Electronic media, on the other hand, bombard us with fast-paced, stimulating sounds and images that have been carefully designed to capture and hold our attention. These sounds and images sort of "wash over us" and leave us with impressions that we don't have time to sort out or consider. That's why understanding how media work and how they affect us is so important. It's so easy to be captivated by television entertainment, electronic games, surfing the Net and popular music. It's important to live intentionally, to consider the trade-offs involved every time we use media (the other worthwhile things we could be doing with our time) and to spend our valuable time only in worthwhile media activities.

General Media Influences

Media can disseminate ideas and worldviews. However, a critical issue to address is, "Whose reality is the media conveying?" There are two factors: media ownership and audience interpretation. Ownership and control of the media and influence on media content cannot be ignored. Yet audiences may have differing interpretations of the message in the content (Chandler 2001:n.p.). In the literacy program,

Bible Societies own the media and have the unique challenge of using the Scriptures as the main text. The audience may include those with little or no exposure to Bible stories. So, it is important to convince the users of the good news that biblical stories tell and point them to the best news of all—the gospel of Jesus Christ.

The combination of different types of media has proven to be effective. The dynamics of combining media can bring across the intended message with greater clarity and effectiveness. However, the excessive use of media, or the use of the highest tech and mosy expensive method is unnecessary. Often, simple and relatively inexpensive methods work just as well, if not better.

There are many advantages of teaching literacy with an audio product. The main advantage is that the audio product becomes the consistent teacher. It contains information and lessons that the learner can listen to repeatedly. Audio production is economical. The other unique traits of the audio product that Søgaard lists are: a person needs only to listen, it is user controlled, readily available, economical (as mentioned earlier), compact, simple to operate, can be used anywhere and anytime—including in private, in the right sequence, repeatedly. It uses limited personal energy. Audio products can be made for specific audiences, local information can be easily added, and local dialects used to teach songs. They can fulfill a particular need as an educational tool, be in a variety of formats, carry a uniform message, be entertaining, and be used as a sound track (Søgaard 1993:161-163).

I mentioned earlier that combining two or more forms of media for groups or individuals can lead to powerful communication. The UBS's forte has been the written Word of God presented in various languages. Bible translations in various countries have been done meticulously and with excellence, keeping close to the original text while using the common language of the people. Even the NRPs are not merely translations from a children's version, or an easy reader, but a true translation that translation consultants have carefully checked for validity.

Perhaps the UBS might develop relationships with radio and television stations who can televise programs for them. In Bangladesh, two Christian studios are at the disposal of the BBS. In Thailand, the Voice of Peace studios, which make professional recordings, have expanded to include video production. In some Latin American countries, local Bible societies get free airtime on secular radio stations (United Bible Societies 2000).

In adapting this program in a new situation, the right media mix for that context should be found. In some cases, audio products will continue to be the best medium to marry with print. In other contexts, it may be more appropriate to develop video, or even computer programs, to teach literacy. In developing countries where resources are scarce, the audio product is still the most viable and affordable option in terms of production costs and effectiveness. It is important to consider the resources available both to the developer and the target audience.

Media Influences on the Development of the Literacy Program

The literacy program in Bangladesh used the audio product and the written primer as a self-contained package that the churches could use with minimum effort and personnel. The method was both high-tech and high-touch. In other words, the literacy program used technology, but not at the expense of de-humanization, or removing the human factor. It acted as a bridge whereby one human being could help another. Past literacy programs, however good, had not produced the phenomenal results of this program. This is a direct result of the media used in the literacy program.

The audio products were audio Scriptures with a consistency and quality control in the communication of the Scriptures and literacy. Program producers carefully selected voices to be personalities that the listener would trust and receive teaching from. They arranged the program format so that the learner did not feel the pressure of learning, but engaged in a natural and fun way with songs and dramas. Producers used local artists, original music and drama. Production costs were relatively low as they used Christian recording studios to tape the master reels.

The other media element—the primer—contained written words and printed pictures. It began with a brief explanation on how learners were to use the audio product and primer together. The learners were encouraged to listen to the audio product and read along in their primers. Since it was also a workbook, the learners could write their answers directly in the book, eliminating the need for an additional notebook. Some of the exercises involved answering comprehension questions, filling in the blanks, free story writing, and even solving mathematical problems.

Although the initial costs of producing the master copy were high, reproduction costs of audio products were low. Likewise, for printing, after the film and printing plates were made, reproduction in large volumes pushed down the price per unit cost.

Adaptation Questions on Media

The adaptation questions to ask toward an effective media mix are:

- What media possibilities are available for use in this program?
- What are the strengths and weaknesses of these forms of media?
- Which combination would be most effective in communicating Scripture in literacy training?
- What systems can disseminate the information (literacy organizations, radio stations, television and social media)?
- How much will it cost to produce and distribute?

Ecclesiastical Context and Its Influence on the Literacy Program

The Church's purpose is to fulfill the mission of God as a witness to people who do not yet know God. Literacy mission should be linked closely with a local congregation. Local churches, as the salt and light of the world, can be the agents of change in society. Christians can build up their witness and good name through a strong missions' program using a combination of social involvement and spiritual presence.

The adoption of a literacy program that brings good news to the poor can boost the mission and overall vision of the Church. It can be used as an instrument to plant a local church, establish new contacts, and serve the community in areas of need. The literacy program acts as a neutral platform where participants become more receptive to the message of the gospel. The program can also serve to disciple followers, as well as develop a leadership program, of the church if needed.

General Ecclesiastical Influences

The local church is located in the midst of a community. Thus, it is an excellent center of operations for a literacy program. It should be a place where people can come freely, find help, and build trust. As a permanent feature of a community, the church offers stability and continuity to a literacy program and provides a platform for ongoing evangelism. In contrast, the efforts of visiting evangelistic teams are often "wasted" where there are no strategic alliances with local churches. In the case study about an evangelistic film-showing troupe, Cinema Leo, presented in one of Søgaard's classes, many who made a commitment to become followers of Jesus later strayed from the Christian faith. Marked changes were seen when Cinema Leo built partnerships with local churches that followed up with new converts (Søgaard 2000).

A church-based literacy program uses the local church, or Christian organization, as the primary agent to carry out the program. The participating church provides a system of delivery for the literacy program. Often the church has a strong interest in using the heart language of the people in the literacy program. It is willing to help the people of the community, but it needs materials for new readers (SIL International–LinguaLinks Library 4.0 2000).

The Presbyterian Church in Malawi was an example of church involvement in the literacy program in the year 2000. Malawi's illiteracy rate was approximately 55 percent of the population. Women constituted 71 percent of the illiterates. The Presbyterian Church in Malawi was not spared the illiteracy problem, which resulted in no women participating in church leadership. The church began a literacy program for women and established a development arm of the church called the Projects Office. By 2000, the church had 42 adult literacy centers open to people of different religions. Women were 95 percent of the beneficiaries (Maloya 2000:1-2).

One unique benefit of the literacy program is that it promotes greater commitment from church leaders and trainers. The church becomes the fertile soil in which seeds of literacy can be planted, tended, and nurtured. A literacy program becomes a means of making and keeping contact with non-Christians. This happened for a church-based literacy class conducted in China:

> The literacy class has had far reaching effects beyond the class themselves . . . class participants have been "set on fire" by their new found skills and have developed a new love and enthusiasm for the church which has given them the gift of reading and writing. Class participants enthusiastically throw themselves in all areas of church work as a way of thanking the church for its gift of literacy. This enthusiasm has spread to all members of the congregation and has given the whole church a new vitality. More importantly, many illiterates from outside the church have heard of this "good thing" the church is doing and are willing to attend the church class in order to learn to read themselves, some hearing for the first time the Good News of the Christian faith (Amity News Service 1998:n.p.).

Ecclesiastical Influences on the Development of the Literacy Program

The success of the program in Bangladesh was attributed to partnerships with local churches. Churches and Christian mission agencies had the resources and vision for a literacy program. The Bangladesh Bible Society's involvement in the literacy program was mainly confined to providing field supervisors who helped coordinate the literacy groups. The working relationship between the BBS, denominations, and the local churches will determine whether churches or organizations will carry the program independently. However, at the beginning stage, a closer partnership and consultation between the two parties was essential. At that time, the churches needed to familiarize themselves with the program and be instructed on how it can be effectively used.

The *Muktir Path* materials were written specially for members of the BLC. The denomination's church leaders expressed the need to give local village pastors and congregational leaders a basic understanding of the Bible. Church members helped create the materials during a script and primer writing workshop. Throughout the process of development and testing of these literacy materials, BLC was the laboratory for experimentation. They provided the literacy groups, as well as the logistics and supervision needed to distribute and manage the program.

After the materials were produced, with all the sets for both *Shukhobor* and *Muktir Path* ready, many other denominations requested that groups be started among their congregations. In order to maintain supervision for their own information and monitoring, the Bangladesh Bible Society employed four men to be supervisors of groups in different parts of Bangladesh. However, these groups were jointly formed with local denominations and churches using a memorandum of understanding. In the memorandum of understanding, the Bible Society agreed to provide training and literacy materials to the churches, while the churches provided the stipend for the local facilitators. The training included a rationale for the program, instruction on how to start and manage the program, and the accountability structure of the program. The local churches chose their own representatives to be involved in the program.

Another concern of the church was the lack of other Christian materials available for new readers to read. They discovered that some Christian missions were producing easy to read materials for devotions and Bible study, as well as testimonial stories. They sourced and made those materials available.

Adaptation Questions on Ecclesiastical Context

The adaptation questions in relation to using the church as an agent for literacy training are:

- Which churches are willing and ready to start a literacy program?
- What should be included in a memorandum of understanding between the Bible Society and the churches?
- What training should be provided to the churches?
- Who should be involved in the program?
- What other Christian materials are available for new readers?

Conclusion

Seven contexts of adaptation have been discussed and analyzed in this chapter. These contexts provide a starting point for the process of adapting the Scripture-focused and media-based literacy program to other settings. The seven principles are:

- Value historical research related to literacy.
- Work with the religious environment.
- Respect sociopolitical norms.
- Be willing to use contextualized cultural forms.
- Create a receptor-oriented educational system.
- Ensure an effective media-mix for literacy training.
- Engage the church as the agent for literacy training.

These seven, considered together in adapting a literacy program to any location, are likened to the roots of a plant in a new environment. Proper consideration, and application, of these contexts provide a firm foundation for further development. As the program takes root in the community, the potential increases for continued healthy growth. The roots will seek out life-giving water and reach deeper so that the plant will grow stronger.

CHAPTER 20

Conclusion

Illiteracy is a global challenge. Defining literacy is difficult, but generally means being able to read and write functionally for self-help and contribution to a community. The challenges of illiteracy are related to hindrances such as low literacy training for women, low motivation towards becoming functionally literate, a lack of suitable materials for new readers, and increasing numbers of children who are not sent to primary school to become literate. Illiteracy poses a direct challenge to the Church as it seeks to minister to people who are unable to read or have limited reading skills; thus, the Church can provide a base for a literacy ministry using Scriptures.

Three famous literacy theorists, Freire, Laubach, and Gudschinsky, and their methods of literacy training offered different literacy principles that were the basis for this project. Combined with audio and print media, these methods could be used create an effective literacy program. Such a program would incorporate motivation, community mobilization, methods of teaching whole language, and the use of media.

Seven contextual influences relate to Bangladesh. These were Bangladesh's rich literary history, pride in its language, national religion that believes in a holy book, government support of literacy, deep cultural heritage, educational system, and secular media support of literacy. In addition, the role of the Church can influence literacy training.

Two perspectives of communication, transmission and culture, led to the conclusion that neither perspectives were sufficient in itself. Communication principles apply to the translation of Scriptures in written and audio forms. Søgaard's comprehensive model can be applied to the situation in Bangladesh.

The experimental project of this book consisted of two sets of materials, *Shukhobor*, for general use among new readers—and *Muktir Path*, which can be used by new readers in the church. These materials can be used by individuals or groups. The unique features of this program were that the materials were contextualized, a system of distribution was established, and logistics were taken into consideration.

The program was developed over an eight-year period. Baseline research began in 1990, ongoing testing and evaluation was done between 1991 and 1994, and a two-year period of monitoring took place from 1995 to 1997. Finally, field research was done in conjunction with this book in 2000. Reading and comprehension evaluations showed a positive increase towards functional literacy (the ability of new readers to read the Bible in the Common Language translation).

In conclusion, illiteracy poses a challenge to Christian communicators that must be confronted. Contextualization will ensure that this literacy project can be adapted to and thrive in many new environments.

References Cited

Abadzi, Helen (1994). *What We Know about Acquisition of Adult Literacy: Is There Hope?* Washington, DC: The World Bank.

Abecassis, David (1990). *Identity, Islam and Human Development in Rural Bangladesh*. Dhaka, Bangladesh: The University Press Ltd.

Adams, Frank (1975) *Unearthing Seeds of Fire*. Winston-Salem, NC: Blair.

Ahamed, Emajuddin, and D. R. J. A. Nazneen (1990). "Islam in Bangladesh: Revivalism or Power Politics?" *Asian Survey*. August, 1990.

Ahmed, Anwar (1990) *Compulsory Primary Education*. Dhaka, Bangladesh: The Bangladesh Observer.

Aid to the Church in Need (1998) "Religious Freedom in the Majority Islamic Countries." 1998 Report, ACN Aid to the Church in Need, Italian Office.<http://www.allean-zacattolica.org/acs/acs_english/report_98/bangladesh>(accessed July 21, 2000).

Akter, A. B. Razia (1992) "Islam in Bangladesh." International Studies in Sociology and Social Anthropology. New York: Brill.

Alam, S. M. Shamsul (1993) "Islam, Ideology, and the State in Bangladesh." *Journal of Asian and African Studies*. Jan.-April, 1993.

Amity News Service (1998) "Church Literacy Class Sets Participants 'On Fire'" October 10. <http://www.amityfoundation.org/ANS/Articles/ans98.10/98>(accessed November 21, 2001).

Arnove, Robert, and Harvey Graff, eds. (1987)*National Literacy Campaigns*. New York: Plenum Press.

Asian Institute of Christian Communication (2002) *The Prodigal Daughter*. Live drama presentation by Christian Communication Institute. July, 2002.

Ballara, Marcela (1999) *Gender Approach to Adult Literacy and Basic Education*. Ankara: UNDP/REKEM.

Bangladesh Bible Society (2001a) "Bible Society Work in Bangladesh." Bangladesh Bible Society, Dhaka, Bangladesh http://www.bible-society.org/bs-ban.html(accessed July 20, 2002).

(2001b) "Literacy Project Involve 100 Churches in the First Five Years." Bangladesh Bible Society, Dhaka, Bangladesh. Report 361 July/August 2001#22 http://www.bible-society.org/wr_361/ 361_22.html(accessed July 20, 2002).

Bangladesh Development Gateway (2001) "Education Policy." http://www.bangladeshgateway. org/sndp/edu/documents/ education(accessed January 10, 2003).

Bangla2000 (2000) "Education." Bangla2000.http:///www.bangla 2000.com/Bangladesh/education.shtml(accessed June 15, 2000).

Barua, Sitangshu Bikash (2001) *Buddhism in Bangladesh*. Original print publication. n.p.:1990. Updated with minor grammatical corrections 2001. Page updated August 13, 2001.http://www. watthai.net/bluws/buddhisminbangladesh. html(accessed Jan. 6, 2002).

Basham, Arthur Llewellyn (1954) *The Wonder That Was India*. New York: Grove Press.

Baxter, Craig (1984) *Bangladesh: A New Nation in an Old Setting*. Boulder, CO: Westview Press.

Baxter, Craig, and Syedur Rahman (1989) *Historical Dictionary of Bangladesh*. Boulder, CO: Westview Press. *Bdtrade Directory* n.d. "National Anthem."http://www.bdtrade-directory.com/ abd/nat_ant.html(accessed March 23, 2002).

BBC News (2003) "County Profile: Bangladesh." <http://www.news. bbc.co.uk/ 1/hi/world/south_asia/ country_profiles/11605>(accessed January 22, 2003).

Bhola, Harbans S. (1984) *Campaigning for Literacy*. Paris: UNESCO.

1994 *Source Book for Literacy Work: Perspectives from the Grass Roots*. Paris: UNESCO.

Bivar, H. (1955)*Literacy in Six Months*. Dhaka, Bangladesh: City Press. Bogod, Elizabeth n.d. "Learning Styles and Multiple Intelligence."http://www.ldpride. net/learning styles.MI. html(accessed February 21, 2003).

Bowman, Jack (2002) *Art Theory and Origin*.http://www.fortune-city.com/victorian/coldwater/234/arttheory.html(accessed September 23, 2002).

Brilla, Anna (1998) "Is Literacy Over-Rated?" March 10.<http://www.aber.ac.uk/media/Students/ alb9601.html>(accessed January 24, 2003).

Burki, Shahid Javed (1986) *Pakistan: A Nation in the Making.* Boulder, CO: Westview Press.

C. Kristina (2013)*10 Countries With the Worse Literacy Rates In the World.* < https://www.care2.com/causes/ 10-countries-with-the-worst-literacy-rates-in-the-world.html>(accessed June 22, 2018).

Chai, Teresa (1990) "Towards Innovations in Non-Print Scripture for Literacy Training." M.A. thesis, Fuller Theological Seminary.

    1995 "Report on Adult Literacy Project." Bangladesh, DMCDO No: MINIP-II, Reg. No. 5, Sept. Photocopied.

    1996 "Report on Adult Literacy Project." Bangladesh, DMCDO No: MINIP-II, Reg. No. 5, Jan. Photocopied.

    2000 "Field Research Report on Media-Based and Scripture-Focused Literacy Program in Bangladesh." Field Research Report. Fuller Theological Seminary.

Chandler, David (2001) "Media Theory." http://www.aberac.un/media/documents(accessed January 10, 2002).

Coombs, Philip (1985) *The World Crisis in Education: The View from the Eighties.* New York: Oxford University Press.

Council for World Mission (2002) "Church of Bangladesh." <http://www.cwmission.org.uk/about/view_ church.cfm?ChurchID=7> (accessed December 2, 2002).

D'Costa, Jerome n.d. "Christianity in Bangladesh." Catholic Bishop's Conference of Bangladesh. no pp.http://www.atma-o-jibon.org/english/christianity_in_ bangladesh.html(accessed May 13, 2001).

Dumont, B. (1979) *After Literacy Teachings: Paradoxes of Post-Literacy Work.* New York: Prospects.

DW Corp Ltd. (1999) "Country Profile: Bangladesh a Gate to the East and the West." Last revised June 29. http://www.epbbd.com/country1.html(accessed June 18, 2001).

Dye, T. Wayne (1980)*The Bible Translation Strategy: An Analysis of Its Spiritual Impact.* Dallas: Wycliffe Bible Translators.

    1986 *Scripture Use Consulting: The Challenge.* Notes on Scripture. Dallas: Summer Institute of Linguistics.

Evangelical Lutheran Church in America Division of Global Mission n.d. "Bangladesh Lutheran Church and Lutheran Health Care, Bangladesh." DGM Country Packets. http://www.elca.org/dgm/country_packet/packets/asia-oceania/bangladesh(accessed July 23, 2002).

Facundo, Blanca (1984) "Issues for an Evaluation of Freire-Inspired Programs in the United States and Puerto Rico."http://www.nl.edu/ace/Resources/Documents/Ohliger1.html(accessed February 12, 2003).

Foothill Leader, The (1991) Picture from Feb. 23, 1991, p. 3.

Franda, Marcus F. (1982)*Bangladesh: The First Decade*. New Delhi: South Asian.

Freire, Paulo 1990 *Pedagogy of the Oppressed*. New York: Continuing Publishing Company.

Goldfarb, Mary Ellen (2000) *The Educational Theory of Lev Semenovich Vygotsky (1896-1934)*. Analysis by Mary Ellen Goldfarb.http://www.newfounda-tion.com/GALLERY/Vygotsky.html(accessed February 10, 2003).

Government of Bangladesh (1999) "Planned Development Relating to Primary and Mass Education in Bangladesh, 1973-1998." Primary and Mass Education Division. Dhaka Bangladesh.

Gudschinsky, Sarah C. (1973) *A Manual of Literacy for Preliterate Peoples*. Ukarumpa, Papua New Guinea: Summer Institute of Linguistics, Inc.

Gustavsson, Styrbjorn (1989) *Primary Education in Bangladesh: For Whom?*Dhaka, Bangladesh: The University Press Ltd.

Haaland, Ane (1984) *Pretesting Communication Materials*. Burma: UNICEF.

Harman, David (1970) "Illiteracy: An Overview." *Harvard Educational Review* 40.

Hart, Andrew (1990-1991) *Teaching the Media: International Perspectives*. New Jersey: Lawrence Erlbaum.

Heaney, Tom (1989) *Issues in Freirean Pedagogy*. New York: Alfred Knopf.

Heitzman, James, and Robert L. Worden (1989) *Bangladesh*. Dhaka, Bangladesh: The University Press Ltd.

Hoekstra, Harvey T. (1982) "Report: Cassette Equipment and Possibilities." *READ* (2):41-42. 1982. *SIL International—*

LinguaLinks Library 4.0. CD-ROM Texas: Summer Institute of Linguistics. 2000.

Human Rights Internet n.d. "Bangladeshhttp://www.hri.ca/partners/forob/e/instruments/asia/bangladesh.html."(accessed December 11, 2002).

Hunter, Carmon St. John, and David Harmon (1979)*Illiteracy in the United States.* New York: Harper and Row.

Jacob, J .F. R. (1997) *Surrender at Dacca: Birth of a Nation.* Dhaka, Bangladesh: The University Press Ltd.

Jacobs, Garry, and Harlan Cleveland (1999) *Social Development Theory* http://www.motherservice. org/Essays/Social DevTheory.html(accessed October 13, 1999).

Jennings, James (1989) *Adult Literacy: Master or Servant?* Dhaka, Bangladesh: The University Press Ltd.

Johnson, Gordon (1996)*Cultural Atlas of India: India, Pakistan, Nepal, Bhutan, Bangladesh and Sri Lanka.* New York: Facts on File.

Joydhor, Richmond (1999*) "Martha Took the Challenge to Literate Her Husband."* Unpublished report for Bangladesh Bible Society.

2000 Interview on April 17, 2000.

Just, Felix (2000) *Journal of Hispanic/Latino Theology* 7.3 (Feb. 2000) 78-80. Loyola Marymount University, Los Angeles, California.

Kabeer, Naila (1991) "The Quest for National Identity: Women, Islam and the State of Bangladesh." *Feminist Review.* Spring 1991.

Kamaluddin, S. (1988) "A Religious Wrangle: Opposition Condemns Moves to Declare an Islamic State." *Far Economic Review.* May 26, 1988.

Kenji, Muro (2000) "What Has Happened to Reading?" September 29, 2000 Berkeley, California. http://www.honco.net/100day/02/2000-0929-muro.html(accessed January 23, 2003).

Khan, M. Ferdouse (1979) "Mass Education in Bangladesh and the Role of Youth." *World Peace Academy of Bangladesh.* Dhaka, Bangladesh: The University Press Ltd.

Kirkpatrick, Joanna (1998) "The Ricksha Arts of Bangladesh." http://www.riksha.org/(accessed September 27, 2000).

Kozol, Jonathan (1978) "A New Look at the Literacy Campaign in Cuba." *Harvard Educational Review.*

Kraft, Charles H. (1997) *Communication Theory for Christian Witness.* Maryknoll, NY: Orbis Books.

Laubach, Frank (1950) *Literacy as Evangelism.* New York: Mohican Press, Inc.

    1960 *Forty Year with the Silent Billion.* New Jersey: Fleming H. Revell Company.

Laubach Literacy (1999) "Frank C. Laubach Founder." http://www.laubach.org/mission/index_ mis.html(accessed February 20, 1999).

Larson, Mildred (1984) *Meaning-based Translation: A Guide to Cross-language Equivalence.* Lanham, MD: University Press of America and Summer Institute of Linguistics.

Lee, Ernest W. (1982) *Literacy Primers: The Gudschinsky Method.* Dallas: Summer Institute of Linguistics. *SIL International—LinguaLinks Library 4.0.* CD-ROM. Texas: Summer Institute of Linguistics. 2000.

Leman, Wayne n.d. "What Does it Mean to be People of the Book?" http://www.geocities.com/bible_ trans-lation/book.html (accessed February 13, 2003).

Lipner, Julius (1994) *Hindus: Their Religious Beliefs and Practices.* London: Routledge.

Literacy Innovations (1996/97) "Technology for Literacy and Lifelong Learning Problems and Possibilities." Fall/Winter 1996-1997. UNESCO Penn International Literacy Institute.

Lonely Planet n.d. "Bangladesh: Culture." http://www.lonelyplanet.com/destinations/indian_ subcontinent/bangladesh(accessed January 29, 2002).

Mackie, Robert (1980) *Literacy and Revolution: The Pedagogy of Paulo Freire.* London: Pluto Press.Majumdar, Ramesh Chandra

    1943 *The History of Bengal.* Dhaka, Bangladesh: University of Dacca.

Maloya, Hastings (2000) "Malawi—Church Initiates Development through Literacy." Malawi: ANB-BIA Supplement, Issue/Edition Nr. 389—1/05/2000.

Maniruzzaman, Talukder (1980) *The Bangladesh Revolution and Its Aftermath.* Dhaka, Bangladesh: Bangladesh Books International.

Mantle, Stacy (2001) "The Seven Learning Styles." Lesson Tutor. May 1, 2001.http://www.lesson-tutor.com/ sm1.html(accessed February 21, 2003).

Martin, Lee R.n.d. "Chart of Translation Theory." http://earth.vol.com/-lmartin/TRANL.HTML(accessed March 12, 2002).

Mascarenhas, Anthony (1986) *Bangladesh: A Legacy of Blood.* London: Hodder and Stoughton.

McLuhan, Marshall (1967) *The Medium is the Message.* UK: Penguin Books.

Merriam-Webster Online (2003) "Translate." http://www.m-w.com/cgi-bin/dictionary(accessed March 16, 2003).

Miller, Valerie (1985) *Between Struggle and Hope.* Boulder, CO: Westview Press.

Moudud, Hasna Jasimuddin n.d. "A Thousand Year Old Bengali Mystic Poetry."http://www.bongoz. com/history(accessed August 8, 2001).

Munslow, Alan (2001) "Introduction." October 2001. www.ihrinfo.ac.uk/ihr/Focus/Whatis history/index.html(accessed November 24, 2001).

National Center for Education Statistics n.d. "Defining and Measuring Literacy." http://www.nces.ed.gov/naal/ defining/ defining.asp(accessed January 10, 2003).

National Formal Education Information Center (1980) *Literacy and Development.* New York: The NFE Exchange.

Nida, Eugene, and William Reyburn (1981) *Meaning Across Cultures.* New York: Orbis Books.

NORAD Norwegian Agency for Development Cooperation (2002) "Bangladesh—Norwegian Agency for Development Cooperation." Last updated September 2002. <http://www.norad.no/default.asp? V_DOC_ID =344>.O'Donnell, Charles Peter (1984) *Bangladesh: Biography of a Muslim Nation.* Boulder, CO: Westview Press.(accessed February 20, 2003).

Ong, Walter (1982)*Orality and Literacy: The Technologizing of the Word.* New York: Routledge.

Open Doors International (2002) "Country Profiles: Bangladesh 2." http://www.gospelcom.net/od/ content/banglapro2.html (accessed February 15, 2002).

Pathania, Joyti M. (2002)"Virtual Diplomacy South Asian Context: Reel or Real?" South Asia Analysis Group Paper no. 572.

December 30, 2002. http://www.saag.org/ papers6?paper572. html(accessed January 7, 2003).

Piaget, Renee (1932) *Piaget vs. Vygotsky: Issues.* http://www.cocoe. k12.ca.us/csuh/edui63000/wk2/vygvsph2.html(accessed November 17, 2001).

Price, Kathryn, and Elizabeth Karr (1985) "Illiteracy: It Can Be Solved through Student and Community Participation." Unpublished manuscript.

Quarishi, Ferdaus A. (1987) *Christianity in the North Eastern Hills of South Asia: Social Impact and Political Implications.* Dhaka, Bangladesh: UPL Books.

Quiah, Philomena (2001) "Da'wah: Invitation from God." *Crossing Boundaries* Fall/Winter 2001.

Radio Netherlands Media Network (2000) "Bangladesh Gets Private TV." http://www.rnw.nl/realradio/ features/html/ekushey 220200.html(accessed February 18, 2003).

Rice, Robert Franklin (2001) Personal interview with author. Tulsa, Oklahoma, April 14.

2002 *World Literacy: Teaching to Read in the 21st Century* 1st edition. Tulsa, Oklahoma: Literacy Ministries International Inc.

Robinson, Francis, ed. (1989) *Cambridge Encyclopedia of India, Pakistan, Bangladesh, Sri Lanka, Nepal, Bhutan and the Maldives.* New York: Cambridge University Press.

Roser Max and Esteban Ortiz-Ospina (2018) "Literacy". *Published online at OurWorldInData.org.* < 'https://ourworldindata. org/literacy>(accessed June 22, 2018).

Sanisoft n.d. "Education Systems."http://www. sanisoft.tripod/ bdeshedu/index.html(accessed August 20, 2000).

Schrøder, Flemming (1993) "Survey of BLC Members." AICC-7 Field Project, Bangladesh, November. Photocopied.

Seventh Day Adventist Church (1995) "A Statement on Literacy" General Conference of Seventh-Day Adventists Administrative Committee, released by the Office of the President, Robert S. Folkenberg, Utrecht, the Netherlands, June 29-July 8, 1995. <http://www.adventist. org/beliefs/main_stat15.html>.haw, R. Daniel (1987) *Transculturation: The Cultural Factor in Translation and Other Communication Tasks.* Pre-publication draft. Pasadena, CA: Fuller Theological Seminary. Shor, Ira

(1987) *Critical Teaching and Everyday Life* (Third printing). Chicago: University of Chicago Press.SIL International—LinguaLinks Library 4.0 (2000) CD-ROM. Texas: Summer Institute of Linguistics.(accessed November 18, 2002).

Smith, Donald (1992) *Creating Understanding*. Grand Rapids, MI: Zondervan Publishing House.

Society for Technical Communication (2002) "What is Communication?" Page maintained by Cynthia A. Lockley. Last revised August 16, 2002. http://www.stewdc.org/communication_answer. shtml(accessed September 20, 2002).

Søgaard, Viggo B. (1991) Unpublished letter dated September 12, 1991.

    1993 *Media in Church and Mission*. Pasadena, CA: William Carey Library.

    1998 Report for UBS. Unpublished report.

    2000 "Survey Research for Effective Communication," MB548/748/848, class lecture. Pasadena, CA: Fuller Theological Seminary, School of World Mission.

    2001 *Communicating Scriptures*. Reading, UK: Reading Bridge House.

Spear, T.G. Percival (2018) *The Mutiny and Great Revolt of 1857-59*. < https://www.britannica.com/place/ India/The-mutiny-and-great-revolt-of-1857-59#ref486238>(accessed June 22, 2018).

Speicher, Sara (2002) Press feature: "The Economics of Evangelism: An Ecumenical Challenge in Bangladesh." Geneva, Switzerland: World Council of Churches Media Relation Office: May 10. http://www.wcccoe.org/pressreleaseen.nsf/4d4fc8b8c54848c1 (accessed June 12, 2002).

Staff correspondent (2015) *Bangladesh's Literacy Rate Rise to 70 Percent.*< https://bdnews24.com/bangla-desh/2015/06/16/bangladeshs-literacy-rate-rises-to-70-percent-education-minister-says>(accessed June 22, 2018).

Sundersingh, Julian (2001) *Toward a Media-Based Translation: Communicating Biblical Scriptures to Non-Literate In Rural Tamilnadu, India*. Ann Arbor, Michigan: UMI.

Sustainable Development Networking Programme (2001) "Bangladesh Female Secondary School Assistant Project." World

Literacy Day. September 8, 2002. http://www. sdnbd.org/sdi/intl_day/lit/docu/ female(accessed February 19, 2003).
"Bangladesh Education Scenario." no pp. <http:// www.sdnbd.org/sdi/intl_day/lit/docu/ status>(accessed February 19, 2003).
"Adult Literacy." http://www. sdnbd.org/sdi/intl_day/lit/docu/adultliteracy(accessed February 19, 2003).

Swim, Gaylord K. (2002) "The Importance of Religious Freedom." Sutherland Speeches. Paper presented as part of the Sutherland Institute 2002 Communication Leadership Program. October 25, 2002. http://www.sutherland institute.org/Publications/SutherlandSpeeches(accessed January 11, 2003).

Tauchi, Yuko (2000) "Who Decides?" Adapted for the web by Paul Black November 28, 2000. http://www.ntu.edu.au/education/csle/student/tauchi/tauchi2.html#3(accessed January 9, 2003).

Tellier, Cherie n.d. "The Importance of the Bible's Representation in Christianity: From the Past into the Future."http://www.ucalgary.ca/~dabrent/380/webproj/cherie.html(accessed December 10, 2002).

Thapar, Romila (1966) *A History of India*. Harmondsworth, UK: Penguin Books.

Tradeport (2000) "Background Notes: Bangladesh." March. U. S. Department of State Background Notes: Bangladesh.<http://www.tradeport.org/ts/countries/bangladesh/bnotes.html> (accessed April 5, 2000).

Trampiets, Fran (2000) "Ask an Expert: The Importance of Media Literacy." October 17. http://www.cnn.com/2000/fyi/teachers.tools/10/16/ask.expert.trampiets(accessed February 13, 2003).

Turner, Peter (1973) "Religion." *United Kingdom: Dictionary of World Religions.*

Uddin, Shehab (2014) *'Second Chance' Education for Children in Bangladesh.* http://www.worldbank. org/en/news/feature/2014/01/27/second-chance-education-for-children-in-bangladesh(accessed June 25, 2018).

UNESCO (2002a) "Estimates and Projections of Adult Illiteracy for Population Aged 15 Years and Above, by Country and by Gender 1970-2015." Updated September 3, 2002. UNESCO Institute for

Statistics. Literacy and Non-Formal Education Sector. July year 2002 assessment.

2002b"Regional Adult Illiteracy Rates and Population by Gender." Updated September 3, 2002. UNESCO Institute for Statistics. Literacy and Non-Formal Education Sector. July year 2002 assessment.

UNICEF (2000) "Bangladesh Basic Education." UNICEF, Bangladesh CD-ROM. 2000.

United Bible Societies (2000) "The Direction from Midrand." UBS World Assembly, Midrand, South Africa, 2000.<http://www.bible- society.org/index2.html>.

University of Maryland, Baltimore County n.d. "Baul—The Folk Music of Bengal." http://www.gl.umbc.edu/~achatt1/baul.html(accessed April 21, 2003).

University of Texas Library Online 2002 Perry Castañeda Library Map Collection, Bangladesh (Small Map) 2002 (17K). <http://www.lib.utexas. edu/maps/cia02/bangladesh-sm02.gif>(accessed March 16, 2003).

Walker, Benjamin (1995) *Hindu World: An Encyclopedic Survey of Hinduism*. New Delhi: Indus.

William Carey College n.d. "Work/Bible Translation."http://www.wmcarey. edu/carey/bib/work_bible.html(accessed March 2, 2001).

World Bank Group, The (1998) "Bangladesh Gives Primary Education a Further Boost with World Bank Support." News release no. 98/1567SAS, no pp. March 31, 1998. http://www.world- bank.org/html/extdr/extme/033198pra.html(accessed April 23, 2001).

The World Fact Book (2018)https://www. cia.gov/ library/publications/the-world-factbook/fields/2103. html(accessed June 22, 2018).

Worldinfomation.com (2000/01) "Media."http://www.worldinformation.com/World/asia/ Bangladesh/profile(accessed February 24, 2003).

Wycliffe Bible Translators n.d. "A History of Bible Translation." http://www. wycliffe.org/hist/ BibleTranslation.html(accessed February 10, 2003).

Zeitlyn, Jonathan (1995) *Appropriate Media for Training and Development*. Dhaka, Bangladesh: University Press Lt.

www.ingramcontent.com/pod-product-compliance
Lightning Source LLC
Chambersburg PA
CBHW070313230426
43663CB00011B/2108